DIEGO MORMORIO

Tazio Secchiaroli

GREATEST OF THE PAPARAZZI

TRANSLATED FROM THE ITALIAN BY
ALEXANDRA BONFANTE-WARREN

HARRY N. ABRAMS, INC., PUBLISHERS

Editor, English-language edition: Amy L. Vinchesi
Design Coordinators, English-language edition: Tina Thompson, Robert McKee

Preceding page: **Tazio Secchiaroli photographed by Gina Lollobrigida**

Library of Congress Cataloging-in-Publication Data
Mormorio, Diego.
   [Tazio Secchiaroli. English]
   Tazio Secchiaroli : greatest of the paparazzi / Diego Mormorio ;
translated from the Italian by Alexandra Bonfante-Warren.
     p.   cm.
   Translation of: Tazio Secchiaroli.
   ISBN 0–8109–4177–5
   1. Photojournalism—Italy. 2. Secchiaroli, Tazio, 1925–1998. 3. Paparazzi—
Italy—Biography. 4. Motion picture actors and actresses—Portraits.
I. Secchiaroli, Tazio, 1925–1998. II. Title.
TR820.M7613   1999
770'.92
[b]—DC21   98–42771

 Harry N. Abrams, Inc.
100 Fifth Avenue
New York, N.Y. 10011
www.abramsbooks.com

In the Farmers' Cisterns

Around 1925, when Tazio Secchiaroli was born there, Centocelle was a cluster of houses in the middle of the Roman countryside, a stone's throw from the imposing, evocative remains of ancient Rome. The small town was surrounded by *marane*—large puddles that the shepherds made to water their sheep—where, in the spring after the rains, children splashed and played.

The beaches of Ostia, which thirty years later would be taken over by Rome's vastly increased population, were, in those days, still far away, especially for the inhabitants of Rome's suburbs. In summer, when the sun turned the *marane* to mud, Tazio and the other children went to beat the heat inside the large cisterns used by the truck farmers for irrigation.

The Secchiaroli family was from the Marches. Tazio's father was the son of peasants who came to Rome in the winter to work in the market gardens. At that time, the city was still surrounded by fields of vegetables and vineyards just outside its walls. Centocelle was

From left: **Tazio at two years old; in the second grade (front row, third from right).**

Tazio at eighteen years old on via Casilina (1943). Below: On a friend's Harley-Davidson (1950).

less than ten kilometers from the center of Rome—only half an hour by train, a very short time compared to how long it takes to cross the city by car today—yet the city seemed very far away. Psychologically, the distance was great. Secchiaroli recalls, "When my mother went to the city, she would say, 'I'm going to Rome.'" Those who lived in Centocelle and the other suburbs considered themselves neither Romans nor countryfolk, and this might explain the motivation behind those who, like Secchiaroli, were children around 1930, and sought in various ways to conquer the city. Before the 1950s building boom ravaged the countryside, it was still almost as Stendhal had seen it in the early 1800s: "The aspect of the country is magnificent: it is not a flat plain; the vegetation is vigorous. Most views are dominated by some remnant of an aqueduct or some tomb in ruins that impress upon this Roman countryside a character of grandeur that nothing can equal."[1] The scenery did not

yet include the film studios of Cinecittà, a major locus of Secchiaroli's professional career. Mussolini inaugurated Cinecittà twelve years after the photographer's birth, on the afternoon of April 27, 1937, with a celebration that included Fascist Party officials, flags, little children in uniform, members of Parliament, and workers, all arrayed in military ranks. The regime's fanfare created an atmosphere which already foreshadowed Cinecittà's sword-and-sandal epics, featuring casts of thousands in far-fetched costumes.

Secchiaroli would enter this "movie city" for the first time as a gofer during the war, in 1943. Because of the gas shortage, it was a time when, to get to Cinecittà and back, famous actors such as Alida Valli, Amedeo Nazzari, Luisa Ferida, and Osvaldo Valenti were obliged to rub elbows with the locals on the train from Rome to the Castelli. When Secchiaroli left this job after a few months, he could not have imagined that it would be

[1] Stendhal, *A Roman Journal* (New York: The Orion Press, 1957), p. 10.

fifteen years before he would return to those "nine hangars surrounded by a wall"—a much longer road than the six kilometers of countryside between Centocelle and Cinecittà. He could not have known that he would return by way of the famous via Veneto and the events of the summer of 1958.

Under the Sign of Sagittarius

Throughout his life, Secchiaroli had always nurtured his dynamic, optimistic temperament, an inclination to be easygoing and jovial, and an uncanny sense of timing. These are all characteristics of the zodiac sign of Sagittarius, under which he was born on November 26, 1925.

A short while before his birth, his parents had used their savings to buy a piece of land on via di Bonifica (today, via Tor de' Schiavi), Centocelle's single street. Tazio's father, a bricklayer, built their house, where Tazio and his two sisters were born, and successfully handed down to his children a strong sense of industriousness. During his summer vacations, Tazio's father ensured he was employed in a manner that would teach him manual tasks, and the familiarity with carpentry and metalworking that he thus acquired had always been a point of pride with him. In 1941, following his father's premature death, Tazio had to leave school. For a year he was a stoker on trains and then, as mentioned earlier, a gofer at Cinecittà.

He took his first photographs that year, using a friend's 35mm Kodak Retina, from the edges of a soccer field in the Centocelle countryside. They were entirely ordinary images that anyone could have taken, yet one of them reveals Secchiaroli's early photographic instincts. Outside the field, the friend who asked Tazio to take his picture is bicycling toward the camera with one of the two soccer goals behind him. As he was about to take the picture, Secchiaroli noticed that the soccer ball, kicked by one of the players, had gone over the horizontal beam of the goal and was coming right at him. He waited until the last minute to shoot, just seconds before the ball hit him. The resulting photograph shows the friend on his bike, next to the flying soccer ball.

In 1944, after he lost his job as a gofer at Cinecittà, Secchiaroli began to work as a *scattino*, i.e., one of Rome's many itinerant photographers who patrolled the train station and the major monuments looking for opportunities. He worked for owners of various photographic materials shops and sometimes for ad hoc employers, who developed and printed their work in improvised darkrooms in old apartments in the historic quarter.

In those months, Rome was full of American soldiers and tourists. Armed with a Rolleicord camera, the *scattino* would wait for them at crucial spots, and then, with a big smile, offer to take souvenir photographs. Many people accepted, surely just for fun; they posed and then received a card with the location where they were to pick up the snapshot. Most simply threw the card away around the next corner or left it in a pocket, forgotten, since they hadn't been asked to pay for it anyway. In the earliest days of this curious photographic activity, the employers—those who supplied the *scattini* with film and cameras—believed that anyone who had their picture taken would of course want to pick it up. After a few weeks, however, reality set in—almost none of the hundreds of soldiers and tourists picked up their photographs. As a result, the *scattinis'* work and thousands of rolls of film have been lost.

Not long after, the itinerant photographers working in Rome were forced to change their methods. Rather than shoot indiscriminately, they would instead approach someone, pretend to take their picture—what was really a fake shot—and if the person seemed interested, the *scattino* would tell him/her to pay twenty lire in advance to get the photograph. Then he offered to take a second shot, just to be on the safe side, and, naturally, it was always the second shot that the clients would see when they went to pick up the photographs. Only a few accepted. By this method, though, the *scattino* saved dozens of rolls of film and took far fewer real photographs. In one day, this amounted to an average of fifteen pictures, which earned him about three hun-

Clockwise: **Tazio at the throttle of a Lambretta, with Luciano Mellace behind him (1952, photograph by Franco Pinna); with a group of fellow *scattini* (1950); in a new suit (1954); and ready for action (1953).**

dred lire after giving the owner of the camera his share.

Once the war ended and the American soldiers went home, life returned to normal and there were once again many tourists. Few of them had cameras, so they were all potential clients. Nevertheless, the itinerant photographers earned just enough to live. During the summer, especially on Saturdays and Sundays, they had to go out to the beaches at Ostia to photograph children, young couples, and families gathered around watermelons.

This was Tazio Secchiaroli's initial experience as a professional photographer, and it lasted for nearly five years, until 1951. In that year, the future *volpe di via Veneto*—"the fox of via Veneto"—became friends with the Roman photographer Luciano Mellace, who worked for International News Service, an American agency that had its office on via del Corso. Thanks to Mellace, Secchiaroli entered the

world of photojournalism, though through the side door: he did small manual tasks, such as helping out in the darkroom and in general filling the role of an assistant.

A now-famous photograph documents this period, which lasted for almost a year. It is a picture by Franco Pinna, who was Secchiaroli's age and would later become another of Italy's most important photographers. It was taken on Tuesday, June 17, 1952, during an anti-American demonstration in the central piazza Colonna, across from the office of the president of the Cabinet and a stone's throw from the Chamber of Parliament. Seen in the foreground from behind, a young man is being taken away by the police; in the background, a photographer, who has just set off his flash, is seated on the back of a Lambretta motorcycle driven by the young Secchiaroli.

"While the arrests were happening," Secchiaroli recalled, "I was driving the Lambretta

and trying to get Mellace three or four meters from the protagonists, so that he could get a picture from the best distance without worrying about being stopped by the police." That picture, along with three others, was published the following day, June 18, in the left-wing newspaper *Paese Sera* with the caption: "From our lens, last night in the center of Rome (exclusive photographs by Franco Pinna)."

Ten years later, however, when the anti-American demonstration was long forgotten, and the mystique of the photographers of via Veneto was taking shape, this photograph began to circulate again, but cropped very differently: gone was the young man photographed from behind, leaving only Tazio Secchiaroli driving the Lambretta with Luciano Mellace setting off his flash. In this format it entered the growing body of work of self-promotion that centered more on the Roman photographers of *la dolce vita* than on the subjects themselves.

Adolfo Porry-Pastorel, Tazio Secchiaroli's First Teacher

In 1988, in his introduction to a book on the photojournalist Adolfo Porry-Pastorel, Tazio Secchiaroli wrote, "He left his mark on me, what psychoanalysts call 'imprinting.'"[2] This statement clearly reveals the significant role that this man played in Secchiaroli's professional training, whose apprenticeship as a photographer began in the agency of this extraordinary character. It is therefore important to understand the personality and working methods of Porry-Pastorel, considered one of the fathers of Italian photojournalism, to gain greater insights into Secchiaroli's success.

The agency's very name bore the imprint of its founder's whimsy: Visioni Editoriali Diffuse Ovunque [Editorial Visions Spread Everywhere], whose acronym VEDO [I see] no doubt had some influence over the choice of the company name.

[2] Introduction, Tita Di Domenicantonio, *Adolfo Porry-Pastorel un fotoreporter leggendario* (Palestrina 1988), p. 7.

Porry-Pastorel was born in 1888 in the Treviso region, of British and French ancestry. His father, an officer in the Bersaglieri, or Italian infantry, died when Porry-Pastorel was only twelve, and so he was raised by his godfather, Ottorino Raimondi, a journalist for the *Corriere della Sera*, and then director of *Il Messaggero* from 1906. It was in the pressroom of this Roman daily, even before Raimondi became director, that Porry—as everyone called him—began to experience "the pleasure of the scent of ink." Even in his earliest days as a reporter, beginning in 1906, the idea of recounting events through photographs was so compelling that he managed to convince the director of the newspaper to let him study the typographic processes involved in reproducing photographs in newspapers. He was then sent to a photo-engraving studio in Germany to master the art of translating photographs into zinc.

Porry-Pastorel's first photographs, which were very well received, were published in the radical-leaning daily newspaper *La Vita*, where he followed Ottorino Raimondi in 1908. His first real scoop, however, wasn't until 1909. One night in Rome, in piazza di Pietra, a couple, Signore and Signora Palmanni, janitors at the Banca Bosio, were murdered. A night watchman discovered the bodies at 4:30 A.M. and Porry beat the police to the crime scene, alerted perhaps by the same watchman. Just two hours later, at seven in the morning, *La Vita* was on the stands with the photograph of the slain couple on the front page.

Porry's situation during the Giolitti administration was golden, at least in terms of the relationship between his work and politics, because the president of the Cabinet liked the "tall, reckless fellow," as he called him. Evidence of this indicates that the day before a private meeting or an important ceremony, Minister Giolitti himself would call to inform Porry of the necessary information. At the appointed time, with the photographer standing in front of him, Giolitti would always exclaim, "This blessed photographer is everywhere; he's persecuting me!"

Soon thereafter Italy entered World War I,

and Porry was on the battlefield, his photographs from the front appearing throughout the world.

The fatigue and hardships that Porry endured during the war failed to diminish his vitality and imagination—he was always ahead of the pack. He proved this yet again on January 3, 1919, on the occasion of United States President Woodrow Wilson's visit to Italy. During the official luncheon, as Wilson sipped his first spoonful of consommé, Porry took a picture. No more than fifteen minutes later, as the waiter served the second course, Porry presented the president with an enlargement of the photograph he had just taken. Wilson rose, went over to the photographer, shook his hand, and said that he would be pleased to meet with him before he left. When Porry went to see him, Wilson offered him a job in America for more than 30,000 lire a month. It was then an astronomical sum, considering the *Giornale d'Italia* paid him 16,000 lire monthly (while the director himself earned only 12,000). Porry put all of his earnings into his agency, Foto VEDO, originally located on via del Pozzetto, and then moved to via di Pietra 87, where it eventually occupied three full floors.

In 1983, during a conversation with students from the University of Rome's Institute of the Performing Arts and Sciences, Secchiaroli, speaking of his debt to and his gratitude toward Porry-Pastorel, said, "In his day, Porry was known as a 'slick' fellow, and his colleagues were wary of him because he pulled stunts, such as pasting stamps on other people's lenses; at the time, cameras weren't single-lens reflex, with direct viewfinders, so you didn't look directly through the lens and you wouldn't notice if something was covering it. Pastorel often used such unorthodox methods to get an exclusive, and so he wasn't very well liked.

"I remember another episode that he told me about, which occurred when Hitler visited Italy. Hitler had gone to Naples to review the Italian fleet, and a twenty-four-hour trip out to sea had been organized. Five or six photographers had been invited along, and Pastorel was one of them. Once on board, the photogra-

Opposite: **Tazio Secchiaroli's first photograph in a small soccer field near Cinecittà, taken in 1943 with a friend's camera.**

Secchiaroli (bottom right) at the Quirinal in 1955.

[3] *Il mestiere di fotografo*, D. Mormorio and M. Verdone, eds. (Rome: Romana Libri Alfabeto, 1984), pp. 47–48.

phers assumed that this time Pastorel wouldn't pull anything because they were all returning to shore together, and would all turn their pictures in at the same time. What they didn't know was that Pastorel had gone aboard a few hours early with a wickerwork suitcase, and inside were twenty homing pigeons, ten from Naples and ten from Rome. When a photographic opportunity arose and everyone started shooting, Pastorel used a Leica—ahead of his time in this respect, as only a few Americans and Germans were using this camera, and

everyone else was still using cameras with plates. Then, at a certain point after getting his shots, he pretended not to feel well, went to his cabin, developed the negatives—he had brought everything he needed with him— attached a frame to each pigeon, and launched them. When the ship returned to port twenty-four hours later, the newspapers were already full of photographs—his."[3]

When Secchiaroli began collaborating with VEDO in 1952, he recalled it was already "an old, rundown agency." But, he added, "it was

Secchiaroli photographing Gina Lollobrigida.

extremely important for me, because it allowed me to get to know an extraordinary person, to hear his stories, and see his photographs: it was a real stroke of luck."[4]

A stroke of luck that came about by chance. A month after the anti-American demonstration where Secchiaroli had driven Mellace on a Lambretta, a VEDO photographer, Mario Tursi, went to the International News Service—where Secchiaroli was then employed—desperately looking for someone to take his place while he vacationed for the month of August.

He asked every photographer there, but no one was available. Secchiaroli, who hadn't been asked—in fact, wasn't a reporter yet—volunteered. Tursi looked at him somewhat doubtfully, then resignedly agreed. He had no idea that within ten years that volunteer would become one of Italy's most famous photographers.

Aware that this was a great opportunity, Secchiaroli was immediately enthusiastic about the new work. Despite VEDO's dilapidated condition, he soon realized the greatness of its founder, whom everyone else spoke of as a

[4]Ibid., p. 48.

13

kind of legend of yore. But the future "fox of via Veneto" wanted to see this legend up close, driven as always by a hunger to learn that characterized his entire life—and which, in more recent years, had urged him to read many, many books during sleepless nights.[5]

When Mario Tursi came back from vacation, Secchiaroli stayed with the agency. On Sundays he often went to Castel San Pietro, one time even spending a week's vacation there, where Porry lived and was mayor, to hear the stories and teachings of one he appropriately considered a master. In so doing he acquired some of Porry's shrewdness, precision, and sense of timing.

Two Italian Stories

Secchiaroli often worked on Sundays for VEDO, photographing soccer matches involving the two Roman teams, Lazio and Roma. He would wait behind one of the two goals for the action to approach, so as not to miss the crucial instant in which the goal-keeper saved or missed the shot. These matches were an important training ground for Secchiaroli, because it was here that he fine-tuned his ability to pay close attention and act quickly.

With that same patience, he spent hours at the editorial offices of *Momento Sera*, where, by contract, VEDO was supposed to have a photographer present at all times. In 1954, Secchiaroli's first famous photographs for his first big scoop were taken for this newspaper.

"One day," he related, "I was at the paper with a colleague, Pietro Brunetti, and they asked for a photographer to go cover a story. There was something strange in the air. I could see that the editors were talking quietly among themselves, trying to keep something secret. In short, I had the feeling that something major was up. So I said to my colleague, '*Pié*, I'll go, do you mind?' He was happy not to go out, and said, 'Yeah, you go.' Then, they took me to the front door of an apartment building, in the Prati area, where the reporter filled me in."

One of the biggest Italian scandals of the 1950s was about to explode. It turned out that there was a brothel in that building, at via

Corridoni 15, where a prominent member of the Communist Party, Giuseppe Sotgiu—an attorney, and president of the Automobile Club and of the Rome provincial council—went to watch his young wife, the painter Liliana Grimaldi, make love with a young accountant, Sergio Rossi, and sometimes with other men or women.

For a time, Signore and Signora Sotgiu hid behind the names "Signor Mario" and "Signora Pia," at least from the stalwart Rossi and their other romantic partners, while the madame of the house knew their true identity. It is almost certain that the police—who in those days kept files on all the leading Communists—also knew. But it is not certain if they were the ones who tipped off the newspaper, as there were undoubtably reporters from *Momento Sera* among the regulars at the brothel.

Hiding himself from view, Secchiaroli photographed Sotgiu entering the building on via Corridoni. Then, after waiting almost four hours, he saw him go out. At this point, Secchiaroli could not photograph him discreetly again, since it was evening and he had to use a flash. Sotgiu noticed him and asked why he was taking pictures, to which Secchiaroli promptly replied that he had recognized him and taken a picture for the archives. Reassured, Sotgiu left, not suspecting that those pictures would soon appear in *Momento Sera*, and later in the weekly *Le Ore*, creating serious problems for the Communists. Although the Communists were as particular as the Christian Democrats about their party members' respectability, they did not perform a background check on the president of the Rome provincial council when he joined the party, because he had been introduced personally by another member.

The scandal was particularly shocking and embarrassing because just a few months earlier, Signor Sotgiu, in defending journalist Silvano Muto in court, had emphasized the immorality and corruption of the bourgeois environment in which the murder of young Wilma Montesi had occurred. Sotgiu's client had attempted to reconstruct this environment in the weekly newspaper *Attualità*, writing about various

prominent upper-class figures, sex, and cocaine, and had wound up in court, accused of spreading "false and tendentious news likely to disturb the public order."

This trial was only a small prelude to the Montesi trial, in which, three years later, Tazio Secchiaroli would find himself playing a role by photographing two of the principals in a fantastic circumstance. The Montesi trial, infamous in those years, could be viewed as emblematic of the hypocrisy, gentility, vice, and dissoluteness that enveloped the lives of a certain segment of Rome's "discreet bourgeoisie." And that brought to the surface certain internal struggles within the ranks of the majority party, as well as the incredible investigative ineptitude of the examining parties.

The Montesi Trial

It all began on the morning of April 11, 1953, when the body of Wilma Montesi, a beautiful young girl with dreams of entering the movie world, was found, naked from the waist down, on the beach at Tor Vaianica.

Immediately, and with no sense of the absurdity of this theory, police headquarters in Rome issued a statement that the young woman had died "washing her feet"; supposedly she had taken off her stockings, put her feet in the water, then, "suddenly taken ill," she had drowned. It would have been difficult to find an explanation more incredible than this one, which went against all the evidence. Wilma Montesi's body, in fact, showed no signs of death by drowning.

The man behind this so-called explanation, Chief of Police Saverio Politi, was an unusual figure in post–World War II Italy. During the Repubblica Sociale di Salò, he was sentenced to twenty-four years in prison for the attempted rape of Rachele Mussolini. Officially, he was a disabled veteran, and had recently received an increase in his pension, due to "a nervous, post-concussion syndrome," which had "rendered the masticatory organs inefficient and [had] caused [him] to limp, his right leg having shrunk by three centimeters."

At the Ministry of the Interior, they apparently knew that Politi's physical condition was not so serious, since Minister Scelba did not remove him from his position. However, twelve days after the right-wing weekly newspaper *Meridiano d'Italia* revealed irregularities in Politi's war pension, officials from police headquarters subsequently confiscated a photographic history of Mussolini that had been public for some time and for which the paper had obtained the consent of the presidency of the Council. These events shed some light on this odd character and the era in which these affairs took place.

Immediately after Wilma Montesi's body was found, word went out that the young woman had been seen in a car with "the son of a well-known political personality," but Montesi's father promptly declared her death an accident. Her mother at first compared her daughter to Maria Goretti (the saint who was murdered after being raped), then, taking the same line as her husband, maintained that Wilma "went to Ostia to take care of her eczema: her footbath killed her." The autopsy revealed that there had been no sexual assault.

At this point, another aspiring actress appeared on the scene. A young society woman from an old Milanese family, Anna Maria Moneta Caglio—dubbed "the Black Swan" because of her raven hair—declared that Montesi had died during a drug-promoted party thrown by Ugo Montagna and Piero Piccioni.

Montagna was a very wealthy real estate consultant with a lavish lifestyle and upper-class friends often of low moral fiber. One of these friends was the pope's personal physician, Galeazzo Lisi, who in 1958 would sell photographs of the dying Pius XII to the newspapers. Depending upon the circumstances, Montagna would claim to be either a *commendatore* or a marquis. (Displaying her deep humility for all to see, Caglio would later say, "I made the biggest mistake of my life when I thought Montagna was really a marquis.") Piccioni was the son of a Christian Democrat minister, Attilio Piccioni, who was close to the great statesman Alcide De Gasperi, and who in those months had been attempting to claim De Gasperi's political legacy. But another political figure was pursuing the same prize: Amintore Fanfani, who, through "the Black Swan's" statements, was identified as the mastermind behind the trial's events.

From the records of Silvano Muto (the *Attualità* journalist), Caglio clearly emerges as Fanfani's pawn: "On November 17, I went to a priest who resides in Rome, to whom I presented all my suspicions concerning Montagna. The priest then verbally informed the Honorable Fanfani. . . ."

The latter's game was simple: to use the younger Piccioni's activities to destroy Attilio Piccioni's reputation, thereby making it easy for himself to become secretary of the Christian Democratic Party. And that's exactly what happened. The trial dragged on until 1957, but only a few months after it began, the Honorable Attilio Piccioni was ruined politically.

Ultimately, after Ugo Montagna and Piero Piccioni, the two principal defendants, had suffered the indignity of prison, they were acquitted of the murder, and the trial ended "Italian-style," that is, without focusing any real attention on Wilma Montesi's death.

During the four years of the case, journalists spilled "rivers of ink." They described the appearance of various seedy characters and reported every tidbit of gossip that came out of their investigations, but they were never seriously concerned with finding out how and why the young woman died. In this context came Tazio Secchiaroli's second photojournalistic scoop—pictures of the two principal defendants, Montagna and Piccioni, in a car.

Secchiaroli recounted: "After waiting for two days in front of the minister's son's house, my collaborator, Velio Cioni, saw Montagna's car drive up; a second later he saw Piccioni come out of the front door of the building and get into the car, which immediately sped off. Cioni followed on his motor scooter. When the car arrived near the stadium, it stopped and Cioni ran to call me. I jumped right into my car and drove to the stadium; the city streets were empty in those days, and you could go from one place to another in just a few minutes. 'Look, they're over there,' Cioni said to me. They had driven into a dead-end street and would have

Piccioni and Montagna, the defendants in the Montesi trial, find the exit blocked by Secchiaroli near the Stadio dei Marmi (Rome, 1959).

to come back the same way. I parked my car so as to block half the street. When they were done talking and doubled back, I blocked the rest of the street with my body. They realized right away that I was a photographer and that to avoid having their picture taken they would have to run me down. And in fact they came right at me, as if they were trying to do just that. But I didn't move. They stopped just a meter away, and I took five or six photographs, which *Epoca* published."

Head Hunters with Lenses

The Montesi trial and the Sotgiu case revealed an Italy that was terribly corrupt and hypocritical, an image that some newspapers tried in various ways to shy away from reporting. Some even blamed the photographers, trying to make them look like the worst part of the whole show. An article entitled "Head Hunters with Lenses" reported a tryst between Signor Rossi—Signora Sotgiu's most frequent sexual partner—and a call girl who was also involved, giving the following account:

"Signor Sergio Rossi and signorina Lucia Carducci had decided to meet in front of the Chiesa Nuova to agree on some of the answers they would give the examining magistrate. Piazza della Chiesa Nuova is a fairly central place, but quiet; however, even if they had chosen a small Trastevere street, or the underground halls of the Palatine Hill, or inside the bronze ball on the cupola of Saint Peter's,

the result would have been the same—they would have run into the photographers. The first four attacked Signor Rossi in piazza della Croce Rossa, as he was getting off one trolley to transfer to another, and the stalwart young man miraculously managed to elude them by climbing into a taxi. At the meeting-place, however, there were other photographers forming a dense crowd, like flies drawn by the smell of honey.

"In front of the Chiesa Nuova, the scenes succeeded each other quickly and absurdly, as in old comic short films: the young man and woman jumped into another taxi to go to any café where they thought they could have a quiet conversation; but in less time than it takes to say, 'Damn those photographers,' hordes of them invaded the place and machine-gunned the fleeing couple with flashes. [Rossi] headed toward his third taxi of the morning, and [Carducci] ran crying into a barbershop.

"Signorina Carducci was a call girl, as they say nowadays, translated from American slang, and appears as such in the Sotgiu affair; she *was* one, but we may imagine that she's lost the taste for it forever. Just twenty years old, with the help of the respectable family to which she belongs, she can still make a new life: she was probably thinking this as she cried beneath the photographers' assault. . . . She'll have to bear up under the examining magistrate's questions, even though she is charged with no crime; but one cannot expect her to adjust to the crude, stupid attacks of young men armed with Rolleiflexes, neither she nor anyone else in the news. It is no longer a question of 'the right to the image,' but of the respect that is due to one's dignity, peace, and even physical safety. Especially since the aggressors reveal themselves to be even more stupid than they are ill-mannered: those photographs, shot en masse and all more or less alike, will compete to be sold to editors for three thousand lire; that's what the 'coup' comes down to."[6] (Photographs that this very newspaper, however, was not above publishing with this article. It was severely critical of the photographers, with a great deal of space allocated to them, and with the eloquent caption "The Accountant's Escape.")

For the writer of the article, Signorina Carducci, "with the help of the respectable family to which she belongs," "can still make a new life" for herself. Her pursuers, on the other hand, have no escape from the criticism. They are destined to remain what they are: "Badly shaven young men, collected from Rome's working-class neighborhoods, or down from the mountains of Abruzzi and Sabina."

Later in the article, the author attempts to find excuses for these photographers, who are simply trying to make ends meet by following more or less pathetic characters around: "In their defense," he wrote, "it must be said that they are acting in the wake of a fashion created by others: the fashion of 'the foreground.' The written news is often no more than a supplement to today's photographic images; where Rolleiflexes and flashes can't reach, the pen can. The significance of an event and even the facts almost disappear behind even minor characters who, in the foreground, become gigantic; their psychological traits are not analyzed, but their clothing—tie, shoes, socks—is described. It is difficult to remain unaware that any given person going down the halls of the courthouse is wearing a suit or a pair of waxed leather loafers. But it may be that the responsibility for this trend lies with society as a whole, rather than with the reporters and photojournalists; and if the news has become

one big gossip-fest we should remember what someone said in the eighteenth century: 'Gentlemen are interested in events, servants talk about people.'"[7]

Picture Hunters

The contemptuously elitist tone of the article also echoed, with varying intensity, in the polemical attitudes of the "dedicated photographers" toward the paparazzi. Most of the former were born into "good" families, and many of them were avowed Communists; they experienced photography as an aesthetic choice and a tool of political struggle. As a result they nurtured a real contempt for the photographers who worked for the tabloids. This point of view, which was shared by many intellectuals, is exemplified in a passage from *Photography and Society*, by Gisèle Freund: "The growing popularity of scandal magazines in Italy during the fifties led to a new breed of photographers called the *paparazzi*. . . . To pry into people's private lives, the *paparazzi* use telephoto lenses. . . . Scandal sheets exist in all capitalist countries. They are known as the 'rainbow press' in Germany, where they are all the rage. In socialist countries, these magazines are considered immoral and cannot be published. . . . Scandal sheets also serve as an outlet for the reader's frustration with life's problems and her envy of those with better luck, for while readers want to daydream about the lives of celebrities, they also want to be privy to every bit of dirt."[8]

In response to these theories, the following points should be considered: (1) Those called "paparazzi" after 1960, that is, after the release of Federico Fellini's film *La Dolce Vita*, were not a "new breed of photographers," but a type of photographer that had been active ever since society/scandal journalism began using photography. More specifically, they are akin to the type of agency photographer of the 1940s and 1950s, the period that Arrigo Benedetti, founder of the weekly newspaper *L'Espresso* felicitously dubbed "the flash age," the age of a photography "without artistic concerns, but is often seen as art," and an age of the "unbiased

A group of photographers, snapped by Secchiaroli, in front of the courthouse during the Montesi trial (1955).

[6] Andrea Rapisarda, "Cacciano teste a colpi d'obiettivo," in *Cronache della politica e del costume* 1, no. 31 (December 14, 1954): 20.
[7] Ibid., p. 22.
[8] Gisèle Freund, *Photography & Society* (Boston: David R. Godine, Publisher, Inc., 1980), p. 181.

Secchiaroli (center) with a group of photojournalists, photographed at the Quirinal (1955).

[9] Arrigo Benedetti, preface to Vincenzo Carrese, *Un album di fotografie* (Milan: Il Diaframma, 1970), p. ix.

photographer," who "wishes to capture reality, and is not concerned with altering it."[9] (2) During the decade of the 1950s, the Italian paparazzi employed regular lenses—and not telephoto—almost exclusively, using flashes and working closely to the subjects they photographed. (3) There has been no scandal press in "socialist countries" not for moral reasons but because there has been no freedom of the press. (4) Various sociological studies have proven that not only does the audience for the society/scandal publications neither detest the milieu nor the people portrayed therein, but it in large measure identifies with them.

The paparazzi phenomenon is complex in a very different way, and may be understood by means of broader reflection.

In 1949, in the introduction to a book of photographs that he edited, Leo Longanesi—at various times author, journalist, newspaper founder and publisher, painter, and graphic artist—very lucidly proved to have identified an aspect of photography that would soon thereafter become glaringly obvious, and that is basic to any understanding of the nature of the relationship between the paparazzo, his subjects, and the audience for his images. "Photography's original artistic intentions," wrote Longanesi, "have now given way to a more documentary-style preference, and, of all there is to be portrayed, what the lens has selected is crime. Corpses are the new favorite motif; a murdered body is the camera's true still life. The beauty of photography has found its

Secchiaroli with Elsa Maxwell at the Bocca della verità (1958).

expression in death by violence. Thus we, too, in the end, become used to seeing corpses, to admiring their tragic postures, discovering, with morbid curiosity, their grimaces and sneers. . . . It has become normal, I might say inevitable, to leaf through a magazine past a murdered body to a beautiful actress in a bathing suit. It is somehow more amusing if the beauty of a female body is transposed with the macabre sight of a dead man.

"Photography does not educate: it corrupts, incites sinfulness, violence, and crime. . . . In short, in photography, flesh, whether dead or alive, is still flesh, pound for pound, though it be butchered flesh. Photography is exciting, perverse, and obscene, capable of bringing mournful images to mind; as a mere profane image, it arouses no thoughts of redemption. Photography is truth—it strips away every illusion."[10]

While Longanesi's description may be extreme and does not, of course, apply to all photography, it nonetheless describes a considerable—perhaps the most significant—portion of it: the part that answers the instinctual human need to view the death of another as a reminder of one's own mortality. Elias Canetti emphasized this in his essay "Macht und Ueberleben" [Power and Survival]: "The terror at the dead man lying before one gives way to satisfaction: one is not dead oneself. One might have been. But it is the other who lies there. One stands upright oneself, unhurt, untouched. And whether he is an enemy whom one has killed, a friend who has

[10] Leo Longanesi, "Il cadavere e il bello fotografico," introduction to *Il mondo cambia, storia di cinquant'anni* (Milan: Rizzoli, 1949); reprinted in *Gli scrittori e la fotografia*, ed. Diego Mormorio (Rome: Editori Riuniti, 1988), pp. 29–30.

Two paparazzi, photographed by Secchiaroli, chasing Ava Gardner's car at 4:20 A.M. one morning in the summer of 1958.

[11] Elias Canetti, *The Conscience of Words* (New York: The Seabury Press, 1979), p. 15.

died, it suddenly looks as though death, which one was threatened by, had been diverted from oneself to that person."[11]

The capturing of death, catastrophe, and violence in its various degrees are photography's principal appeal, its answer to the public's deep, unconscious need to know that one is safe in the face of another's struggle or defeat. This type of disturbing photograph cannot help but fascinate people. For these same reasons the public is particularly attracted to scenes in which famous people attempt to escape the photographer's gaze: the struggle by which these people pay for their celebrity with the loss of their privacy demonstrates a vulner-

ability that at once distances them from and yet brings them closer to the general public. The fiercer the celebrity's struggle, the more enthralled the public becomes. In many ways this has turned the photographer into a hunter of faces and gestures, pursuing and then capturing his prey.

In a September 1958 article in the magazine *Epoca*, Secchiaroli, remarking on the exploits of a group of paparazzi, said, "Now, there's our target, our face: who's going to let it get away? Obviously, on these occasions, nothing will stop us, even if it means overturning tables and waiters, or raising shrieks from an old lady who doesn't quite get what's happening; even if it means shocking John Q. Citizen—he's always there—who protests in the name of the rights of man, or, conversely, galvanizing the other citizen—also ubiquitous—who takes our side in the name of the freedom of the press and of the Constitution; even if the police intervene or we chase the subject all night long, we won't let go, we'll fight with flashes, we'll help each other out. . . . The increasingly ruthless competition means we can't afford to be delicate; our duties, our responsibilities as picture-hunters, always on the lookout, and pursued ourselves on every side, make it impossible for us to behave otherwise. Of course we, too, would like to stroll through an evening, have a cup of coffee in blissful peace, and see via Veneto as a splendid international promenade, rather than one big workplace, or even a theater of war." [12]

Secchiaroli's use of the phrase "picture hunters" and description of via Veneto as a "theater of war," expressed perfectly the feelings of the paparazzi. Another time, the photographer frankly admitted, "Of course, there was some resentment on our part. The luxury, the American cars, the ready cash. At the time, I was earning fifteen hundred lire a day, absurdly little. . . ." [13] And, even more explicitly, he added another time, "We had nothing, and they, the rich men who were living *la dolce vita*, had everything: beautiful women, cars, money. . . ."

For the paparazzi, therefore, photography became more than a battle for economic survival: it became a battle, period. As such, it was also an internal battle of wills against the secret pleasure of the struggle and the need for affirmation.

Photographers under Attack

Ironically, Secchiaroli's initial fame arose from one of these battles. It began with a squib in the Milanese daily paper *Il Giorno*, which appeared on the front page on Tuesday, August 19, 1958, and was titled "Photographer Attacked by Farouk and Franciosa."

"A photographer," the article related, "had a dramatic experience last Friday night on via Veneto, when he was attacked, first by ex-king

Farouk of Egypt, and then by an actor, Anthony Franciosa. It all began at 2:00 A.M. on the night of Ferragosto on the 'Left Bank,' at the Café de Paris, whose clientele of society nightowls is augmented every evening at that hour by the ex-sovereign's considerable presence. King Farouk, in summer wear (light-colored trousers and white shirt-jacket) had collapsed onto a chair, surrounded by a small entourage made up of Irma Capece Minutolo, familiar to society columns as the colossal ex-king's almost constant companion, Minutolo's sister, [14] and the Neapolitan Mario Ottieri, father of 'Gennarino Pascià,' who married an Indian princess.

"At one point, a total of five photographers fanned out near the ex-king, all set to begin the almost nightly scrimmage that Farouk usually seems to greatly enjoy. Not so last Friday night. With the only relative agility that his weight allowed, the ex-king leapt up and hurled himself at one of the 'reporters,' Tazio Secchiaroli, who freed his camera from the ex-king's embrace and then tried to wriggle out of it himself. The intervention by Farouk's around-the-clock bodyguards was providential: they intervened on behalf of their protégé, but in fact saved the photographer from hand-to-hand combat.

"While Mario Ottieri, for all his monarchism, was sneaking out of the fray, and King Farouk was fleeing to the most remote room of the Café de Paris, a police unit forcefully intervened, and the photographers took off for good. They were not so much driven away as drawn away to the 'Right Bank' by Ava Gardner's arrival with Anthony Franciosa, the leading man in *The Naked Maja* and, they say, the current leading man in Ava's fickle heart.

"The couple was going into the Brick Topo and again it was Tazio Secchiaroli who arrived and set off his flash. Anthony Franciosa's reaction was the same as Farouk's earlier one: he immediately hurled himself at the photographer, with even more energy and with greater agility. This time it was the other photographers who waded in to rescue their colleague, as Franciosa lacked the necessary bodyguards.

"Ava and Anthony went into the nightclub and came out more than two hours later, at

Top:

King Farouk and Irma Capece Minutolo (on his right), photographed by Secchiaroli at the Café de Paris on the night of August 16, 1958.

Bottom:

Anthony Steel and Anita Ekberg in front of a group of photographers that includes Secchiaroli (photograph by Massimo Ascani).

[12] Tazio Secchiaroli, "Li fotografiamo e loro ci picchiano," in *Epoca* 9, no. 414 (September 7, 1958): 53.
[13] *Il mestiere di fotografo*, op. cit., p. 46.
[14] According to Irma Capece Minutolo's testimony, it was not her sister, but another woman.

Above and opposite: **Secchiaroli in the infamous confrontation with Walter Chiari (1958, photograph by Elio Sorci).**

[15] Ivo Meldolesi owned an agency whose office was on via Due Macelli. His collaborator, Pierluigi Praturlon, who would later use his first name only, would be the set photographer on Federico Fellini's *La Dolce Vita*. He also took one of the photographs that inspired scenes in the film.

exactly 4:30 A.M., she with her press agent, David Hama, he with a truly disarming smile for his 'friends' the photographers. Thus, like all stories, this one, too, had a happy ending."

Five days later, on August 24, in a smoother, less breathy tone than that of the *Giorno* reporter, the weekly *L'Espresso* (among the most influential papers in those years) picked up the same item in a half-page article entitled: "Ferragosto in Rome: That Terrible Night on via Veneto."

Thus, two small news items started to create a myth, with a cast of characters that seemed to join past and present: a king, bodyguards, female companions, police officers, photojournalists, and movie stars.

But what really happened on the night of August 15, 1958?

After a dinner suffused with wine from the Castelli Romani, Secchiaroli and three other photographers—Bonora, Guidotti, and Pierluigi—were going home by way of via

Veneto. As they passed the Café de Paris, Pierluigi, who was driving, slammed on the brakes, saying, "There's Farouk! Let's get out!" In their summer euphoria, this common routine suddenly became fun. Pierluigi stopped the car in the middle of the street, rushed out, and began photographing the former king of Egypt from around the flower bed in front of the bar; Guidotti did the same, but came around from the other side, while Secchiaroli jumped over the flower bed, and, making his way between chairs, set off his flash right in Farouk's face.

The ex-king was used to photographers' flashes, and usually rather liked being photographed, but—as the episode was recalled by Irma Capece Minutolo, then Farouk's young companion and later his wife—he was startled by the suddenness of the action, and believed it to be an attempt on his life. Hence the ensuing scuffle that made the photographers' sortie famous. However, without *Il Giorno*'s front-page article and *L'Espresso*'s smaller mention, it likely would have gone unnoticed, or only appeared in some gossip magazine. In the summer night life of Rome, it was an almost banal event.

The most poignant era of clashes between photographers and celebrities began in 1949. The director Roberto Rossellini and the Swedish actress Ingrid Bergman, in the midst of their affair, were making a film on Stromboli. No one in Rome had seen them together. One evening, acting on a tip, Ivo Meldolesi and a collaborator, Pierluigi Praturlon, tracked them down at a restaurant near Porta Pinciana.[15] "They managed to get some pictures secretly before Rossellini took notice, and, out of the blue, threw a plate of spaghetti at the two photojournalists. In the ensuing turmoil, Rossellini fled the restaurant, followed by his companion. Pierluigi, who had miraculously dodged the plate of pasta, quickly straddled his motorcycle and caught up with the director at his apartment building, on via Bruno Buozzi, to try to photograph the couple going in. As Rossellini crossed the threshold, however, he noticed the photographer and, in an unexpected maneuver, managed to trap him, closing him into a

corner of the entryway, keeping him not only from taking pictures, but also from leaving. Pierluigi remained captured that way until a tenant, drawn by his shouts, freed him and let him go."[16]

From that day on, these kinds of photographic skirmishes became increasingly frequent, as more and more actors came to work in what would be dubbed "Hollywood on the Tiber." This film world attracted two or three thousand girls each year in search of fame and fortune, girls who, as one journalist put it, given "the sexy tone of Italian films" were inclined to "consider any nonphysical qualities as mere accessories to acting."[17]

In 1958, such confrontations with photographers reached their peak with the Farouk and Franciosa incidents, and later with Anthony Steel.

"Steel," Secchiaroli recounted, "was leaving a nightclub with Anita Ekberg. I got close to take a picture, but he rushed me. There was no call at all for it, it was a peaceful situation. I realized right away that he was drunk. I remember, it was three in the morning, via Veneto was completely deserted, it practically looked like something out of De Chirico: just one policeman, the driver, another photographer, and me. Steel became furious and jumped me. The situation was almost comical, because as I ran away, weaving between the tables, I would photograph him, throw a chair behind me, and he would trip over it."

The most famous and deliberate collision, however, remains the one between Secchiaroli and the actor Walter Chiari. "One evening," the photographer recalled, "we were following Ava Gardner and Chiari, who were nightclubbing around Rome. There were four of us: Elio Sorci, myself, and our collaborators. We had taken pictures of the two of them going in and out of nightclubs, worthless photographs because there were so many just like them. So, later, as he was parking and she had gone to open the door to the apartment building, I told Sorci to get ready. Then I went up very close to Gardner and set off a flash in her face; she screamed and Chiari immediately rushed me.

Sorci promptly started shooting and got some pictures in which it looks as if we were fighting."

The pictures were published with a great deal of fanfare in the magazine *Settimo Giorno*, and subsequently made the rounds of several newspapers.

"In situations like this one," Secchiaroli added, "we discovered that by creating little incidents we could produce great features that earned us a lot of money. That way we could break the humiliating barrier of earning only the three thousand lire from the newspapers for a photograph, and instead earn as much as two hundred thousand lire."

At the same time, the idea spread among those in the entertainment world that to challenge the photographer's gaze—even to pretend to do so—was to create an episode that very likely would end up in the newspapers, adding to their celebrity. Some stars even informed a photographer of their movements ahead of time, so they could be sure to be "surprised" when one came upon them. Thus, a considerable number of the so-called *paparazzate* were in fact setups, performances on the part of both photographers and celebrities. Contrary to what has often been said, therefore, what distinguished the paparazzi was not that they invented a photography of societal scandal, which has almost always existed, but that they introduced a methodological variation into it. By transforming the photographic moment into a kind of provocation, they also transformed it into what was really self-representation of the photographer. Thus, in the *paparazzate*, the photographer also became a celebrity, the very center of the photographic act.

The Age of Flashbulbs and Fiat 600s

Walter Benjamin declared that the decisive element in photography remains the relationship between the photographer and his technique. The paparazzo's technique was embodied in the Rollei's twin-reflex system, as in the Rolleiflex, or the less expensive Rolleicord. A sturdy, medium-format camera, it had a bulky Braun flash attachment that was slow to

[16] Andrea Nemiz, *Vita, dolce vita* (Rome: Network edizioni, 1983).
[17] Mario Tedeschi, *Roma democristiana* (Milan: Longanesi, 1957), p. 98.

recharge from its heavy lead battery, which was carried from the shoulder.

Thus equipped, the paparazzi were far from inconspicuous, especially since they had to work very close to their subjects. This made their provocation technique the most appropriate to their photographic technology, especially in the context of street photography. They were unconcerned with aesthetics, and yet they unconsciously created an aesthetic that was specific, essential, and a perfect reflection of the world from which these photographers came—an Italian working-class milieu, with little formal education, but much skill in getting by.

Not having jobs in government offices, the paparazzi nonetheless tried to avoid working very much; many were able to remain true to this ideal throughout their lives. Once he was able to afford to do so, Tazio Secchiaroli worked just until he tired of the job, "Just a third or a quarter of the year." He dedicated the rest of his time to strolling the boulevards and to reading voraciously, curious as he was about a vast variety of subjects.

In the early 1950s, Italy was slowly becoming more prosperous, but it was still a poor country: only 7.4 percent of homes had electricity, drinkable water, and indoor plumbing. A far greater number of people were employed in the agricultural sector than in any other field. According to the 1951 census, 42.2 percent of the population lived on "agriculture, hunting, and fishing." In the south, the figure was 56.9 percent.[18]

At that time Italy also was a country of emigrants. Between 1946 and 1957, more than 1.1 million people left Italy for the Americas. Seventy percent of them were from the south, and many of them were day laborers. Nearly 400,000 of them never returned.

Thanks to low labor costs, Italian industries of the period were able to gain significant shares of the international markets, jump-starting the country's industrialization and what would be called its "economic boom." Between 1954 and 1963, the net Italian gross national product almost doubled, rising from 17 billion lire to 30 billion lire. Per capita income increased from 350,000 lire to 571,000 lire. The number of people employed in the agricultural sector decreased by about 3 million, while the number of people employed in industry reached 40 percent of the population, with 35 percent in the public services sector. In short, changes in production began to alter the face of the country.

In 1952, only 500,000 cars circulated in Italy, but there were many more motorcycles, especially Vespas and Lambrettas. In 1953, the car manufacturer Fiat made an enormous capital investment in a gigantic assembly line to produce the Seicento, or 600, model, which entered the market in 1956, inaugurating the era of mass motorization in Italy.

As a result, the exploits of the paparazzi were soon accompanied by the roar of Vespas and Lambrettas, and later by the Seicento.

Roma Press Photo Agency and Secchiaroli's Celebrity

Tazio Secchiaroli had owned a Lambretta since 1951, but in 1956, the year the Seicento appeared on the market, he bought a car.

He was now beginning to do very well as a photographer. Almost a year before, he had founded, with Sergio Spinelli, the Roma Press Photo agency. The partners divided the work according to their gifts: Secchiaroli, naturally, was the photographer, while Spinelli, who had been at Pastorel's agency, where he and Secchiaroli had met and become friends, was in charge of marketing and public relations.

Roma Press Photo's first office was in an apartment on via Nazionale occupied by a group of painters who provided the partners with a room and a kitchen, which they used as a darkroom.

Initially, Secchiaroli and Spinelli worked at least twelve-hour days, usually the former at night and the latter by day. In the late afternoon, Secchiaroli went to via Veneto, and then returned home at dawn after developing and printing the night's pictures. Spinelli, on the other hand, began work when the newspapers' editorial offices did; he made telephone calls and solicited features from potential clients;

[18] Cfr. Paul Ginsburg, *Storia d'Italia dal dopoguerra a oggi. Società e politica 1943–1988* (Turin: Einaudi, 1989).

The article in the magazine *Oggi* (January 28, 1960), in which Secchiaroli related the days of *la dolce vita*.

with a picture of Secchiaroli, followed by the shot of Walter Chiari pursuing the photographer. Most significant about this spread was that Secchiaroli's name appeared with those of some of the most celebrated photojournalists. In its January 28, 1960, issue, the paper *Oggi* published an article signed by Secchiaroli: *Ho fatto a pugni con Faruk in via Veneto* ["I Had a Fistfight with Farouk on via Veneto"]. Shortly thereafter, the photographer's fame spread internationally, as he appeared in *Paris Match* and *Time* magazines. In October 1962, he was invited to take part in a debate televised by the RAI on his experiences on via Veneto—a period thereafter dubbed *la dolce vita*—along with Arrigo Benedetti, director of *L'Espresso*, the actor Walter Chiari, and an attorney, Giuseppe De Gennaro. At that point, Secchiaroli was not only the most famous Italian photographer; he was truly *the only* famous Italian photographer.

among the first were such magazines as *Le Ore*, *Settimo Giorno*, and *Settimana Incom*, and soon included prestigious publications such as *L'Europeo* and *L'Espresso*.

In only two years, Roma Press Photo garnered a considerable portion of the market. In 1957, they had to move to new offices and hired on two more collaborators, Velio Cioni and Giovanni Lentini. In 1960, they had twelve employees.

It was also thanks to Roma Press Photo's organizational strengths that Tazio Secchiaroli soon became a famous photographer. Just one month after the memorable Ferragosto episode in 1958 and *Il Giorno*'s front-page article, the weekly *Epoca* published a six-page article by Secchiaroli in the September 7, 1958 issue entitled *Li fotografiamo e loro ci picchiano* ["We Photograph Them, and They Beat Us Up"]. There followed a feature in *Settimo Giorno*, with the infamous incident of the actor Walter Chiari chasing Secchiaroli, photographed by Elio Sorci.

On November 6, 1959, the weekly paper *Rotosei*, in the second part of a feature on the "history of photographic journalism," opened

Fellini, Creator of the Paparazzo Mystique

Tazio Secchiaroli would not likely have achieved the fame he did, however, were it not for Federico Fellini's film *La Dolce Vita*, which created both the word "paparazzo" and the mystique of via Veneto, which was only partially rooted in the actual reality of the street's daily life.

"During my nerve-wracking search for a producer for the film," Fellini wrote, "while I was doing preproduction work and before my fortunate encounter with Angelo Rizzoli, I had found one man who demanded *Via Veneto* as a title. Still today, many reporters, especially American ones, call me, begging me to introduce them to the intellectual and erotic rites that they believe begin and end on via Veneto. The more unscrupulous of them say they'll spend whatever they have to, they promise to be discreet, and they insist that I bring along Anita Ekberg. When I reply that I can do nothing, that I don't know the password to the world of 'Roman holidays,' no one believes me. They would believe me even less if I told them the truth, which is that in my movie I invented a via Veneto that doesn't exist, exaggerating and molding it with the freedom of fantasy to the dimensions of a large allegorical fresco."[19]

An exaggerated, molded, and allegorical via Veneto. But also a street whose day-to-day reality made room for Fellini's brand of allegorical expression.

An excerpt from one of the *Fogli di via Veneto*, by the author Ennio Flaiano, who wrote the subject and screenplay for *La Dolce Vita* with Fellini and Tullio Pinelli, enhances this: "June 1958. With Fellini and Tullio Pinelli, I'm dusting off an old idea for a film, the one about a young man from the provinces who comes to Rome to be a journalist. Fellini wants to bring it up to date, depict this 'café society' that flits between eroticism, alienation, boredom, and our [Italy's] sudden prosperity. . . . One of our locations will have to be via Veneto, which has increasingly become one big party; tonight I took a walk there for the purpose of seeing it clearly. How different it is from the 1950s, when I went there on foot every morning, across Villa Borghese, and I would stop at the Rossetti bookstore with Napolitano, Bartoli, Saffi, Brancati, Maccari, and Cardarelli the poet. The air was clean, the traffic was peaceful (Brancati traveled around on a bicycle), the aroma of hot brioches wafted from the baker's shop, there was a cheerful local atmosphere, journalists and writers drank their aperitifs, painters didn't have galleries, people flew less. I used to meet Mario Soldati at the barber shop, and he would say 'I'm writing a novel.' How a street can change! Now that summer is almost here, it's very obvious that this isn't a street anymore, it's a beach. The cafés that overflow onto the sidewalks. . . . The cars slip like gondolas to the theater, in brief jolts, and the public enjoys the cool air, walking up and down with the indolence of algae and the false assurance of choristers. . . . The conversations are like those at the seaside, baroque and jocular, referring to an exclusively gastro-sexual reality. All that is missing is the splash of the sea and the volley of a beach ball."[20]

Just sixty years earlier, on this site of "seaside conversations," was located Villa Ludovisi, the most beautiful villa in Rome, which so enchanted Henry James that he wrote about it

in his *Portraits of Places* (1883). In lush detail, he recounted the fantastic lawns and gardens surrounded by the great wall of the city, the shadowy walks and vast landscapes shaped by centuries of rolling hills and valleys, forests and pastures, fountains overflowing with reeds, and resplendent flowered fields dotted here and there with enormous leaning pines. He dubbed the villa a revelation, with a view of the city's bastions enjoyed from the gardens above the trees, flowers, and climbing plants.

In 1887, construction fever spelled the demise of this magnificent place. In its place rose the Ludovisi neighborhood, whose center was via Veneto. The neighborhood was originally inhabited by the lower middle class, while the wealthier class lived nearby in large apartment buildings just constructed on the Esquiline Hill. It was not until some thirty or forty years later, however, that the upper classes began to discover via Veneto as a result of its transformation into "the center of hotels and the meeting place of the exotic."[21] Just behind the attractive store windows, however, were still the traces of the neighborhood's celebrated origins: dark staircases, outdoor water closets on the inner balconies, and malodorous courtyards. As late as the early 1950s, a flock of sheep might still be seen crossing town in the middle of the night, as late-night patrons were leaving the clubs.

Fellini's Debt to the Photographers

Secchiaroli's celebrity and the paparazzi mystique were largely due to Fellini's film *La Dolce Vita*. Conversely, the director owed many ideas for certain key scenes of his memorable movie to the photographers.

"I spent," Fellini recalled in the summer of 1962, "a number of evenings chatting with Tazio Secchiaroli and the other photojournalists of via Veneto, learning the tricks of their trade. How they spotted their prey, how they teased them, how they tailored their features for the various newspapers. They had hilarious stories of lying in wait for eternities, of imaginative escapes, and of dramatic chases. One evening I decided to take all the photojournalists I

Secchiaroli on via Veneto in the summer of 1958 (photograph by Velio Cioni).

[19] Federico Fellini, "Fellini presenta la storia di via Veneto," in *L'Europeo* 18, no. 27 (July 8, 1962): 59.
[20] Ennio Flaiano, *Opere. Scritti postumi* (Milan: Bompiani, 1988), vol. 1, p. 623.
[21] Silvio Negro, *Roma, non basta una vita* (Venice: Neri Pozza Editore, 1962), p. 250.

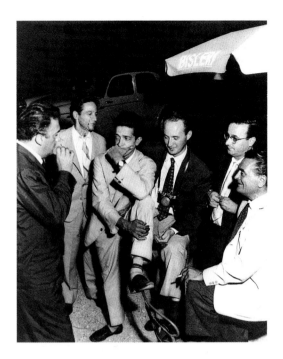

With Federico Fellini at dinner at the restaurant Gigetto er Pescatore (November 1958).

[22] Fellini, op. cit., p. 60.
[23] Diego Mormorio, "Pierluigi. Dalla dolce vita in su," in *Photo Italia*, no. 159 (September 1988): 82.
[24] A couple of weeks later, these pictures appeared in the magazine *Tempo illustrato*; along with those of the assault on Farouk, Walter Chiari chasing Secchiaroli, the miracle in Terni, and the striptease at Rugantino, they made a profound impression on Fellini.

met to dinner, and I confess that, inspired by the white wine of the Castelli Romani, they told me a lot of tall tales, until Secchiaroli said, 'Stop making up nonsense, you're carrying coals to Newcastle.' At the time, I didn't know whether to take that as a compliment or an insult." [22]

The dinner took place in November 1958, in a restaurant near the Milvian Bridge, called Da Gigetto er Pescatore. Among the photographers along with Tazio Secchiaroli were Guglielmo Coluzzi, Ezio Vitale, Sandro Vespasiani, and Pierluigi (Praturlon).

A few months earlier, Pierluigi, who would later be the set photographer for *La Dolce Vita*, had taken some photographs that inspired Fellini's scene of Anita Ekberg bathing in the Trevi Fountain.

"Anita and I often went out together," Pierluigi recalled. [23] "We used to go dancing at a place near Casalpalocco. One night in August, in 1958, Anita, who always danced barefoot, hurt her foot. Coming back to Rome at four in the morning, we passed the Trevi Fountain and Anita said, 'Stop the car so I can rinse my foot.' 'No, come on,' I said. 'You'll be home in five minutes.' She insisted, so we stopped. She got out and, hiking up her skirt, began wading into the fountain, at which point I got my camera and started shooting her in the fountain's dusky glow. I remember two carabinieri standing in a corner who weren't more than twenty years old. They didn't say a word. They were completely entranced watching this beautiful woman in the fountain, with her long, lovely legs." [24]

Fellini's scene in the film depicting the miracle, however, was inspired by pictures by Secchiaroli. On a slow day in the summer of 1958, Sergio Spinelli was leafing through the newspapers, when he came across an item in *Il Tempo* about two children in Terni who had seen a vision of the Virgin Mary on a tree. He asked Secchiaroli to go and take a look. He resisted, but Spinelli insisted that he go.

Latteria di Maratta Alta, the location of the apparition, was an open space surrounded by a few cottages. Secchiaroli had no intention of returning to Rome empty-handed, given the distance he had traveled, and he soon realized that there was much to be done if he were to get some usable photographs. So he tracked down the children and convinced their parents to dress them in their First Communion finery. He then took them to the site of the supposed vision, had them kneel, and encouraged them to re-create an ecstatic reaction. Little by little a small crowd gathered. Soon, the photographer knew he had the image he was looking for: the two children praying to the tree in the foreground, surrounded by twenty or thirty gaping peasants.

Though the feature sold easily, the matter was hotly debated for several weeks. In the end, the Church declared that what had taken place was not a miracle, but only a combination of the fantasies of two children, popular credulity, and a photographer's inventiveness.

The Striptease at Rugantino

The photographs that inspired the striptease scene in *La Dolce Vita* were taken by several photographers, including Secchiaroli. When they were published in the November 16, 1958, issue of the weekly paper *L'Espresso*, they triggered a scandal that led to the confiscation of the newspaper and a public outcry. The following article provides some insights into the debacle: "Rome. The panic began on Thursday afternoon. It was a little past noon when hundreds of telephones began to ring urgently on the Parioli, in the villas of the suburbs, in the palazzi of old Rome. On the line were representatives of Roman café society who spend their evenings in the nightclubs around via Veneto, including actors and actresses, young industrialists and rich heiresses, painters and variety-show artists. Still groggy from their evening activities and subsequent lack of sleep, their exchanges—some long-distance—were confused and excited. The news reached as far as Turin, Genoa, and Milan that Aiché Nanà, a Turkish dancer, had performed a striptease the previous night at a private party at Rugantino, a restaurant in Trastevere.

"But what really happened at Rugantino on the night of Wednesday the fifth? To answer this question, one has to know first of all who threw the party that took such an unexpected turn: Olga di Robilant (everyone knows her as Olghina) is twenty-five years old, very tall, blonde, and from an old Venetian family. Like many girls of the Italian aristocracy, both rich and poor, Olghina wanted to work to both feel independent and avoid boredom. But whereas so many others in this position look for work as secretaries, interpreters, or salesgirls in a designer's shop, Olghina decided to become an actress. In fact, she had already had a small part in Fred Zinnemann's *Nun's Story*.

"Olghina believed that the shortest distance to celebrity was publicity; getting your name in a newspaper or, even better, your picture, was worth more than a thousand smiles at a director or two years in acting school. As up-to-date about the goings-on in the international film world as any girl in her position could be, Olghina got the idea for the means to her end from something that happened in Rome two weeks ago. A party given by Marc Doelnitz, a Frenchman known only on the Left Bank in Paris, was reported, with photographs, in a number of weeklies. Why? Doelnitz's party had intrigued the press not only because of the important people who attended, but especially because it represented something new, something already the case in France: aristocratic names mixed with those from the worlds of film, theater, literature, and painting, the more modern and unconventional the better. Olghina decided to take a leaf from that book. However, being neither very rich nor very well known, she turned to her friends for help. She turned to Peter Howard Vanderbilt, an American millionaire, to split the cost of the buffet and of renting the restaurant.

"All the guests arrived on time, and the mix of artists and society achieved on Wednesday night at Rugantino was even more successful than the one at Doelnitz's house, a welcome break in a boring stretch that had been running since the beginning of the social season. The death of Pius XII had contributed to this, and even the party that the Belgian ambassador, Van der Elst, had given at Villa Doria-Pamphily in honor of Prince Albert, King Baldwin's brother,

who had come to Rome for the coronation of the new pope, hadn't lifted spirits.

"Early on, however, Olghina's party seemed nothing more than a failed attempt to interrupt a long series of boring affairs. The scotch, roast chicken, and roast beef were not enough to bring Rugantino to life. Rather than dance, many preferred to sit and listen to the Roman New Orleans Jazz Band, Italy's most famous jazz group. Nor was the monotony relieved by Peter Howard Vanderbilt's rude expulsion of a blond, balding American of about thirty-five, who left unprotestingly. 'He's a writer for *Confidential*,' said Vanderbilt, 'and a real traitor. He was a good friend of mine, but two or three years ago he sold me out to that scandal sheet.'

"Even the arrival of Anita Ekberg and Linda Christian went almost unnoticed in the dimly lit room. The young American was with two Roman friends; her blonde wig contrasted sharply with her black pearl earrings. The Swedish actress, in a black velvet dress, wore her long hair loosely over her shoulders. Anita, noticing the gathering boredom in the smoky room, immediately accepted Jacques Sernas's invitation to dance; she was apparently the only one willing to do something to liven things up. She asked the photographer Gerard Hearter to partner her in a Charleston and danced so vigorously that she fell down twice during her dizzying spins. At that point, a brown-haired woman who had been in the corner until then, and whom few had noticed, got up from her chair and went over to the band. The trumpet and saxophone drowned out what the girl said to the drummer, Peppino D'Intino; apparently her request was unusual, because the musician looked perplexed. A few minutes later, however, he began a drum solo, and the young brunette began to dance by herself.

"No one paid much attention except for Anita Ekberg, who asked Novella Parigini if the girl might be beginning a belly dance. 'I think she's a specialist, a professional dancer,' the actress said to the friends at her table. At this point, the woman had stopped dancing, but Novella Parigini went up to her to deliver Anita's suggestion. Parigini was turned down, as

A waiter brings pizza to photographers seated on the stairs at the Osteria dell'Orso.

Secchiaroli with the actress Barbara Valentin at the 1959 Venice Film Biennial.

[25] *L'Espresso* 4, no. 46 (November 16, 1958): 12–13.
[26] Mimmo Pacifici, "Così cominciò la dolce vita," in *Gente Mese*, October 1988, p. 114.

she said she wasn't dressed properly—to do the Oriental dance requested of her, her stomach had to be bare.

"Novella Parigini went back to Anita and whispered in her ear, but gradually the conversation between the two women became louder. If the brown-haired woman would take off her white dress, the actress proposed, she would do the same, but she wouldn't be the one to start. By now the rumor of an impromptu striptease was going around the rooms, and all the guests who had been chatting in low tones ran into Rugantino's main room. Something new and different was finally about to happen. 'It was about time,' said a young man from the south. 'It was getting unbearable.' It was as if someone had opened a window in an airless room.

"When the unknown young woman noticed that she was suddenly the center of attention, and flattered by the encouragement of a famous actress who had never seen her before, she climbed onto the band's platform.

"First, she requested a rug, because the belly dance cannot be performed on just any flooring. Her request was immediately fulfilled when some young men took the napkins off the tables and spread them over the bricks. The stranger said that wasn't enough; she wanted to dance on a floor of men's jackets. A rather hefty man around thirty years old was the first to drop his dark jacket among the sauce-, lipstick-, and wine-stained napkins. More jackets rained down and the carpet was ready.

"The drum rolled, as the drummer tried to coax the sound of a tom-tom from his instrument. After a couple of whiskies, the girl put her hand on her hip, and touched the zipper on her dress.

"A second later, her clothing was sliding to the ground, and the girl was left wearing only her black lace panties. Continuing to go with the rhythm of the drum, she slowly took off her stockings, one after the other, then threw them languidly into the audience.

"The belly dance was short-lived. The owner of the restaurant had retained two plainclothes police officers to keep an eye on the ladies' jewelry, and they proceeded to stop the dance and ask the gathering to break up. The guests crowded at the door. The last one out was Aiché Nanà, the girl who had danced half-naked, a girl who had come to Rome to make movies. She left alone because her escort had already departed, in order to avoid problems with the police. She was crying, wrapped up in an old coat. The next day the police charged her with indecent exposure."[25]

The Context

The evening of Aiché Nanà's striptease, there were four photographers besides Secchiaroli at Rugantino: Frontoni, Sarsini, Palotelli, and Guidotti. They all stayed close to the scene, photographing the dancer almost exclusive of the crowd. With a sharper photographer's eye and sense of framing, Secchiaroli instead climbed onto a table a few meters away, so as to get a better shot of the dancer as well as her surroundings. He alone understood, almost instinctively, that the appeal of the event also included, to a significant degree, the presence of all those "respectable" society people; the lusting gazes of the men who had laid their jackets on the ground to make a carpet for the dancer; and the other women's half-smiles and slightly perplexed expressions. "What was happening before my very eyes," the photographer said, "was indescribable in those days, the most sinful, transgressive thing I had ever photographed."[26]

Secchiaroli was well aware that he was photographing more than a girl taking her clothes off. The event put in context was truly shocking. *L'Espresso*'s feature observed: "The other night, around the naked Turkish woman, were men and women anchored to the solid beliefs of social preservation." These beliefs allowed them to take for granted "the conviction that they have a right to their own morality."

Secchiaroli managed to shoot the entire striptease by using his film sparingly, and with his flash half-charged, so as not "to be left in the dark during the best part." Now and again he

caught disapproving glances from Anita Ekberg, who was next to him.

When he finished the first roll, he went out and hid it in his car to avoid its being confiscated by the police, who had been called by the owner and were on their way. During the exiting stampede at the end of the party, he took out the film left in his camera and passed it to a press agent, Lucarini, who "took it safely away."

The pictures of that evening wound up in *Life* magazine, as well as other foreign magazines, and that was how the Roman *dolce vita* became established as an international phenomenon even before the release of Fellini's film. But only Fellini would be able to re-create the psychological, social, and cultural atmosphere so magnificently.

The writer Alberto Moravia, in a review of Fellini's work, would say, with some far-sightedness: "In Fellini's *La Dolce Vita* the very fact that the reporter Marcello Rubini has no philosophical stance—when, as a professional, he should be equally interested in all news-worthy events, from the appearance of a celebrity to a supposed miracle on the outskirts of Rome—suggests how today's news

With Princess Paula of Liège (1960, photograph by Paolo Pavia).

measures and blends everything in a manner that is characteristic of modern city life.

"On the other hand, Marcello's life is very similar to the newspapers in which he publishes: it has neither head nor tail, it is absurd, empty, and gratuitous, lacking fullness and activity. Thus, Marcello Rubini is a felicitous invention because he is not some harsh judge who takes a step back and condemns, but rather an actor-spectator who contemplates his mistakes in the very moment he makes them, a little like the first-person narrator in Petronius' *Satyricon*, a fictionalized record of the *dolce vita* of an age in many ways like our own.

"It is not by chance that we cite Petronius. They say that Fellini is a Catholic; no doubt he is, in his own way, but first and foremost he is decadent in a baroque sense, one whose camera is trained on material very like the Latin writer's. By this we mean that Fellini, perhaps unintentionally, has been able to capture with fresh insight that Alexandrian quality that modern society shares with the society of Petronius' time. All the aspects of what we are calling Alexandrian are in *La Dolce Vita*: sexual promiscuity, latent mysticism, cruelty, laziness, the desire for taboo pleasures, cosmopolitanism, aestheticism, irrationality, and so on. It matters little that the society Fellini describes is, necessarily, limited to a few hundred people in via Veneto and its environs. Fellini was quite right to describe it as if it were wholly representative, because it is: firstly, as a direct product of modern culture, and, secondly, as simply the Italian offshoot of a much vaster international society."[27]

Moravia's reading of the film's narrative structure is profoundly illuminating. "With *La Dolce Vita*," he went on, "Fellini has made his best film and one of the most meaningful of the last several years, because he has succeeded in finding the best narrative model for his talent. . . . *La Dolce Vita* is so much more vast, richer, more resonant than his earlier films, and this might suggest that Fellini is best served by an 'open' narration, that is, with no plot and no beginning or end; based not on a logical, coherent development, but rather on infinite repetition. Petronius' *Satyricon* is another good example of this narration, with neither beginning nor end. *La Dolce Vita* lasts three hours, yet is rendered so weightless and delightful by the director's extraordinary skill, that it could easily be two or three times as long. This quality confirms Fellini's decadence in a technical sense as well; it knows nothing of limits or symmetries."[28]

In this great, decadently refined fresco of a society that in its impetus to evade boredom becomes shipwrecked between major and minor events, all equally insignificant, the photographer is, in the end, the figure in which this loss of direction and sense of emptiness are most apparent. In Fellini's *La Dolce Vita*, the paparazzo's shamelessness feeds off of a world that has lost any sense of perspective.

The Origin of the Word "Paparazzo"

"A coarse society, which expresses its cold lust for life more through exhibitionism than by really enjoying life," noted Ennio Flaiano, during the period when he was writing the subject and screenplay for *La Dolce Vita*, "deserves shameless photographers. Via Veneto is invaded by these photographers. There will be one in our film, the protagonist's inseparable friend. The character is very clear in Fellini's mind, a prototype based on an agency photojournalist that he told me an awful story about. This guy had been assigned to the funeral of a famous person who had died in an accident to get a picture of the widow crying. But, due to some oversight, the film was exposed and the photographs didn't come out. The director of the agency said, 'Work it out. Bring me the crying widow in two hours or I'll fire you and sue you for damages as well.' The reporter rushed to the widow's house and found her just returned from the cemetery, wandering from room to room, stunned with sorrow and fatigue. To make a long story short, he told the widow that if he didn't get a picture of her crying he would lose his job, and with it any hope of getting married, as he had recently gotten engaged. The poor woman wanted to throw him out, as you can imagine how disin-

[27] Alberto Moravia, "Il 'Satyricon' di Fellini," in *L'Espresso*, 6, February 14, 1960, p. 23.
[28] Loc. cit.

L'EUROPEO

872 - ANNO XVIII - N. 27 - SPED. IN ABB. POST. - GR. 2ª   SETTIMANALE POLITICO D'ATTUALITÀ   L. 100 - 8 LUGLIO 1962

Federico Fellini presenta

LA STORIA DI VIA VENETO

I fatti e i personaggi di una strada famosa raccontati dal regista della «Dolce vita» attraverso uno speciale documentario fotografico

clined she was to stage her grief, after crying so much for real. But the photographer went down on his knees, pleaded with her to be kind, not to ruin him, to cry for just a minute, even just pretend, as long as it would take to get a picture. He succeeded. The poor widow, weakened by pity, let herself be photographed crying on the couple's bed, at her husband's desk, in the living room, in the kitchen."[29]

After this unflattering portrait of the kind of photographer that the film would feature, Flaiano added, "Now we had to give this photographer a meaningful name, because the right name helps a lot and gives the character life. These kinds of semantic affinities between characters and their names drove Flaubert mad: it took him two years to come up with Madame Bovary's name, Emma. We didn't know what to call our photographer, until we happened to open George Gessing's brilliant

Cover of *L'Europeo*, 1961: *Federico Fellini presenta la storia di via Veneto* [Federico Fellini Presents the Story of Via Veneto].

[29] Ennio Flaiano, "'La storia di via Veneto,' alla ricerca della strada perduta," in *L'Europeo* 18, no. 28 (July 15, 1962), repr. in Ennio Flaiano, *Opere,* op. cit., vol. 1, p. 630.

L'EUROPEO

SETTIMANALE POLITICO D'ATTUALITÀ

ANNO XVIII · N. 28 · SPED. IN ABB. POST. · GR. 2º   SETTIMANALE POLITICO D'ATTUALITÀ   L. 100 · 15 LUGLIO 1962

Continua il grande documentario

LA STORIA DI VIA VENETO

La famosa estate del '58

book *By the Ionian Sea*, and therein found a striking name: 'Paparazzo.' Thus, we decided the photographer will be called Paparazzo, never knowing that he bears the honored name of a hotelier in Calabria, of whom Gessing speaks with gratitude and admiration. But names have their own destinies."[30]

So did George Robert Gissing's, which Flaiano inadvertently misspelled, and subsequently in certain photography books became set as Gessing. In *By the Ionian Sea*, the 1909 account of the English author's travels, Coriolano Paparazzo is the proprietor of a hotel in Catanzaro who learned "with extreme regret that certain travellers who slept under his roof were in the habit of taking their meals at other places of entertainment. This practice, he desired it be known, not only hurt his personal feelings, but did harm to the reputation of the establishment."

Unlike what Flaiano wrote, Gissing expressed neither gratitude nor admiration for the hotelier, but merely said, " the fare provided by Signor Paparazzo suited me well enough." That is all Gissing wrote about the Calabrese hotelier in his book, which came out in an Italian edition (published by Universale Cappelli, under the title *Sulla riva dello Jonio. Appunti di un viaggio nell'Italia meridionale*) in December 1957, right around the time Fellini, Flaiano, and Tullio Pinelli were writing the subject and screenplay for *La Dolce Vita*.

Although Gissing wrote Signor Paparazzo's service "suited" him, in fact, it becomes evident to the reader that the hotelier's demand that his patrons be loyal to his establishment is absurd, a kind of presumption not unlike that of the photojournalists operating around via Veneto. But this is not why his name was given to the photographer in the film who shadows the protagonist, played by Marcello Mastroianni. Rather, it was because phonetically, the name has pejorative connotations, which for Fellini and Flaiano were appropriate for the character, played by Walter Santesso.

These connotations arise from the suffix *-azzo*, a variant of *-accia*. The latter is currently used in Italian to "reinforce a pejorative"

(*Dizionario Garzanti della lingua italiana*); for example *donnaccia, figuraccia, fattaccio*, and so on. Although it is rarely used in northern Italy, *-azzo*, with the same value as *-accio*, is still used in contemporary Italian—for example, *amorazzo*, a love affair—and is commonly used in southern Italy.

In this sense, "Paparazzo" is a paradigmatic name. It has, to quote Flaiano again, "semantic affinities" with the character who bears it. It was not, therefore, a chance selection, but instead the felicitous creation of a label now used throughout the world.

Roll 'em! (and let the fun begin)

There was a period when it looked as if Tazio Secchiaroli himself might play the part of Paparazzo. On March 15, 1959, the weekly paper *Lo Specchio* wrote, "The inclusion in the cast, in the part of the photojournalist, of one of the best, most skillful, and unscrupulous Italian picture-hunters currently on the scene—Tazio Secchiaroli—is currently under discussion."[31]

By the time the first *La Dolce Vita* story board was viewed in studio 14 at Cinecittà, on March 16, at 11:35 A.M., everyone knew that Fellini had decided to cast the actor Walter Santesso in the photographer role, who was in character in his very first sequence—number 206. Pierluigi Praturlon was on the set, representing the photojournalists of via Veneto. "The film's photojournalists (Santesso, Doria, Cerusico, Paradisi)," wrote Tullio Kezich in the notes heading the film's screenplay, "began to take shape. For several weeks, they had studied how to use the cameras and flashes, and now they moved with practiced ease. Pier Luigi Praturlon, the set photographer, in a black-and-white-checked beret and fake buckskin jacket, was right behind them. As soon as a sequence was shot, Pier Luigi would howl like a drowning man: 'Photograph!' That would start off a game that was to continue for the duration of the film: the technicians would pretend to ignore him; Martelli, the camera operator, would threaten to turn out the lights; and Fellini would shout picturesque insults at him. But it takes more than that to stop Pier Luigi's drive."[32]

[30] Loc. cit.
[31] Paolo Pavia was also rumored to be under consideration for the part.
[32] *La dolce vita di Federico Fellini*, Tullio Kezich, ed. (Bologna: Cappelli editore, 1960), p. 41.

Opposite:

La storia di via Veneto in three issues of *L'Europeo*, 1961.

La storia di via Veneto continues.

Secchiaroli appeared on the set on the second day of filming to say hello to Fellini. Kezich noted, "Today another photojournalist, Tazio Secchiaroli, came by. It is he who provided Fellini with a number of original ideas for *La Dolce Vita*." For this reason, the author gave a thumbnail sketch of Secchiaroli, and he became a significant presence in Kezich's important book on Italian cinema: he is quoted several times and appears in three photographs.

Thus, Secchiaroli's name became inextricably linked with the director's. "After that, Fellini believed that I brought him luck. So whenever he began a new film, he always called me," Secchiaroli said.

The great master of the film *8½* had realized that Secchiaroli, besides bringing him luck, was unique among the photographers of via Veneto. His intelligence and creativity clearly distinguished him from the others.

From Paparazzo to Set Portraitist

Following his new success and refined talents, Secchiaroli soon stopped working as a street photographer, and, after *La Dolce Vita* came out, gave up his nighttime forays.[33] He clearly had the gifts to become a "legitimate" photojournalist, but given the choice, he was inclined to follow his passions to the fantastic milieux of film sets.

He began as a set photographer, but became an artist. Between takes he captured the glances and gestures of film personalities, shaping a gallery of beautiful portraits that is at the same time a series of fantastic works of art.

An episode in February 1961 confirmed his low regard for the world of journalism, especially Italian journalism. In the evening of New Year's Day, Secchiaroli was in Moscow as set photographer for Alessandro Blasetti's film *I Love, You Love*. The cast had been invited to a party at Domkino film institute. Among the guests was Bruno Pontecorvo, the great Italian nuclear physicist who had moved to the USSR ten years earlier for political reasons. Secchiaroli immediately recognized Enrico Fermi's former assistant, around whom were gathered a few high-profile members of the Italian Com-

munist Party. Arousing some surprise, he pulled out his old Leica—"I bought it in 1954 from a taxi driver for sixty thousand lire, two months' salary"—and started to take pictures. The result was an interesting feature, with a touch of scoop, as there had been very few photographs of Pontecorvo since he had been living in the Soviet Union, and those few were almost institutional. A month later, L'Europeo published Secchiaroli's reportage, with a banner headline on the front page.

The article that accompanied the images was written in such a way as to suggest that the writer, who had not been in Moscow that night, had also been at the party. The writer merely repeated the photographer's account, but without directly quoting him. Secchiaroli's name appeared below the journalist's name, and in smaller type.

This infuriated the photographer, who had had another bad experience with the same

paper in 1957, also surrounding an event in the Soviet Union. In that year, the "Youth Festival"—organized by the Communists in a different socialist country every year—was held in Moscow. Secchiaroli, taking advantage of an inexpensive travel opportunity, had gone to see the city and had photographed various young Muscovites trying to buy Western-style clothing from their counterparts from the other side of the Iron Curtain. When he went back to Italy, he offered the pictures to L'Europeo. The director, Giorgio Fattori, "looked me in the eye," Secchiaroli recounted, "and said, 'You mean to tell me that you go as a guest to a foreign country and show its worst side?' " Whereupon he bought the feature and never published it.

Secchiaroli was not political and had no hostile intent toward the socialist countries, but he learned from that experience how broadly photographs can be interpreted, and that this material was very sensitive, particularly in Italy.

Left: **Pages from L'Europeo (July 29, 1962).**

Right: **Pages from the book with the screenplay of Fellini's La Dolce Vita (edited by Tullio Kezich for Cappelli editore in 1960) in which Secchiaroli appears with some of his pictures.**

[33] "After Fellini's La Dolce Vita," Secchiaroli said, "anyone in Rome with a camera went to via Veneto to look like a paparazzo. There was a mob of photographers."

Secchiaroli's Pontecorvo scoop in Moscow (*L'Europeo*, March 1961).

34 *Il mestiere di fotografo*, op. cit., p. 48.

Paradoxically, his Pontecorvo scoop led him in a different professional direction, to a kind of photography in which the record of a film set becomes a genuine poetic reality, suspended between the materiality of the characters and the dreamlike quality of the scenery and backdrops.

This vision began to take shape around 1960. Around that time, Secchiaroli was beginning to refine his great photographic instinct to encompass more of the unexpected, happenstance quality of events within his very specific, all-embracing vision of photographic reality. His work was along the edges of a merry dream world, almost utopian, what was for him like returning to a happy childhood.

His experience with Fellini's *La Dolce Vita* was a pivotal one, as was his meeting with renowned photographer Gjon Mili. Like seemingly all significant encounters, it happened by chance during a screen test for Martin Ritt's *Jovanka e le altre*. Mili, on an assignment for *Life*, was slowly working around the set in intense concentration. Secchiaroli had no idea who he was at first, but when he found out he became very excited and began to pester the American master with questions and devoted attention. Finally, after a few days, Mili agreed to take Secchiaroli on as an unpaid assistant, and Secchiaroli dropped all his commitments to do so. For three months, during the making of Ritt's film, Secchiaroli followed Mili around, carefully noting the great master's choices, trying to understand the sculptural qualities of light, the merit of out-of-focus foregrounds, the compositional qualities of the background. And soon he made his most radical discovery to date.

"We were in the mountains of Austria," Secchiaroli recounted. "Every now and then, Mili would make me stop so he could take pictures; at one point, in front of a little church, he took his camera, changed the lens, and lingered longer than usual, shooting. I didn't understand what was so interesting; when I asked him, he replied, 'You see, God is bigger than the mountains.' Using a wide-angle lens, he made the church larger and the mountains smaller. In that moment, a window opened. I said to myself, 'This guy thinks before he takes a picture.' For me, photography was only movement, action, a fast, instinctive thing, a gesture, in other words, via Veneto. But Mili used his head." [34]

From then on, Secchiaroli cut himself off from his paparazzo past and took a different route, focusing his new photographic skills on two people in particular: Federico Fellini and Sophia Loren.

Federico . . .

For Secchiaroli, Fellini represented the beginning of a new life, the discovery of the wide world of fantasy and imagination: "If it weren't for Fellini," he said, "I might have remained a paparazzo. He opened the doors of Cinecittà to me, but more than that, he showed me things I never would have understood on my own. Watching him, I learned to see the world in a disenchanted and slightly amused way. It was as if I had taken a load off my shoulders, or rather, off my brain." Thereafter, Secchiaroli worked on each of Fellini's sets, with the exceptions of *Juliet of the Spirits* and *Orchestra Rehearsal*.

During preproduction of the film that brought them together, Fellini asked the photographer to use a flash to shoot various candidates for a part, and to foreground them. "At the time," Secchiaroli recalled, "his request seemed odd. I would have been inclined to do portraits with more suitable lighting. But he said that he absolutely wanted them with a flash, with the same light that the via Veneto photographers used during their nighttime forays. I guessed the reason for his request years later, just as I realized much later how good *La Dolce Vita* was. The first time I saw it, I didn't like it. I thought it was a movie without a story. Only later did I understand that that was what made it beautiful. I was still a via Veneto photographer, and the only thing I had in common with Fellini was an ordinary, mutual human affinity. We liked each other right away, from the first time we met at the restaurant da Gigetto er Pescatore. I immediately felt an instinctive admiration for Fellini, and a faith in him."

He would manifest his faith in the director in a difficult moment.

"When it looked as if we would never find a producer for *La Dolce Vita*," the photographer recalled, "and when he saw me indiscriminately printing photographs of locations and aspiring actors, Fellini asked me mischievously, 'Hey, Tazio, who's paying for these pictures?' Convinced that he would find a producer sooner or later, I replied, 'Someone will pay me for them.'"

Secchiaroli's calm smile as he expressed his optimistic belief, brought Fellini—who had a superstitious streak—to trust the affection that ultimately bound him to the photographer. Fellini was completely relaxed in front of Secchiaroli's lens, and that allowed him to be totally himself—a peerless performer.

"He was," the photographer said, "a volcano, constantly erupting with funny one-liners. When you were on the set, it was like being at the circus. It looked like chaos, but everything worked perfectly. He knew how to get people to follow him, like a great orchestra conductor. That led me to concentrate my lens on him, rather than on the scenes of the movie. I was interested in what he was like, in his personality. It occurred to me that in reality, he was the star of the show. It's that simple."

Secchiaroli's focus proved very apt on the set of *8 ½*, where the photographer's interest in Fellini as a character coincided perfectly with the film's strongly autobiographical theme. The result was the finest portrait of the director of his entire career—*un passaggio obbligato* for anyone studying the master.[35]

. . . and Signora Loren

After *8 ½* was completed, Marcello Mastroianni, with whom Secchiaroli had become very friendly during the filming of *La Dolce Vita*, mentioned the photographer to Sophia Loren, with whom the actor was preparing to film *Marriage Italian Style*. It was 1964.

"Signora Loren," as Tazio had always addressed her, brought him onto the set, and, after ten days of filming, she in turn received from him a splendid series of photographs.[36] Sophia Loren, who certainly knew something about photographs, was so impressed that she telephoned the photographer personally to tell him how much she admired them, a truly great compliment for someone in Secchiaroli's position, who after all was just doing his job.

Top to bottom: Tazio Secchiaroli in a portrait by Gina Lollobrigida (1971); with Fellini on the set of *Amarcord* (1974, photograph by Pierluigi); on the set of *Intervista* (1987).

[35] Secchiaroli acknowledged that he only truly recognized the significance of this work some time later. He came to understand that, in Fellini's oeuvre, *8 ½* was a much better film than *I vitelloni*—the film that he especially liked—and that it represented a fundamentally significant moment in the history of the cinema in the last fifty years.
[36] Secchiaroli recalled: "I had taken some of what I consider my best photographs."

Top to bottom: **Secchiaroli** on the set of *Marriage Italian Style*; with Sophia Loren on the set of *Bianco, rosso e . . .* (1970).

Opposite:

Sophia Loren and Tazio Secchiaroli.

[37] Sophia Loren, Introduction, in *Tazio Secchiaroli: The Original Paparazzo* (Milan: Photology, 1996).

The actress, who, like every great diva, liked to be the last one to come onto the set, told him, "I detest people who arrive after I do, but you may come when you like. You are an artist." Thus began a twenty-year collaboration, during which Secchiaroli photographed the actress in various moments of her private family life as well.

"With *la Loren*," the photographer said, "I really understood what light is. Few people have as good a sense as she does of this basic, incorporeal thing. But that's not all. *La Loren* is one of the greatest people I have ever known. Beneath the diva is a simple, generous woman who, out of her great sense of fairness, detests cynicism, slyness, and arrogance."

In turn, the actress has described Secchiaroli in terms that are beautifully insightful. "Beneath an apparently cold and inattentive expression," she has written, "Tazio has the instinct and controlled aggressiveness of the true photographer, one who will take a hundred or even a thousand shots until he is sure that he has got exactly the one he was looking for. Above all, Tazio has one great talent: he never pesters you, he will not confuse you with suggestions, he never tries out sterile experiments. Like a good hunting dog (I hope Tazio will forgive the analogy, but I do love dogs), he does not run or jump without reason. With all his senses on the alert, he waits patiently for the precise instant, however fleeting it may be, to seize the picture and freeze it forever on his film."[37]

Tazio traveled all around the world with Sophia Loren. He rubbed elbows with the most famous actors and directors, but always remained the simple boy who came from the outskirts of Rome. His relationship with the actress ended only when he decided to retire from photography altogether. "Because," he said, "photography, like any art, requires a great deal of energy. In 1983, I felt that this energy was exhausted. So I decided to quit."

Postscript

For almost twenty years, Tazio Secchiaroli and I shared a friendship of mutual esteem and affection which never lacked the reserve, modera-tion, and respect that so many of today's relationships are missing. I met him when I was writing my thesis, and it struck him as odd that a student of literature and theology would also study photography. Our friendship sprang from this, our mutual curiosity about our differences.

At the time, I was accustomed to most of the photographers I met thinking they could change the world with their photographs, but I immediately saw Tazio as a man swimming against the current, who sought only to understand the world. For him, photography, besides being a way to "earn a living without working too hard," was, he said, "a way into other people's psychology." He was very intrigued by what he called "intellectual photographers," but he couldn't understand their "obsession with publishing books." He himself had no desire to publish a volume of his work, saying "There are already so many books." Each time I proposed such a volume, he would laugh and repeat this phrase. Acknowledging the tides of destiny, I would reply "Fine. When the time is right, we'll do it."

Of course, the time came just when I had given up hope. To my great delight, Tazio brought out the boxes of his photographs, and, with his son David's help, we began making our selections. As expected, he approached the process with his usual coolness. But in the end, when he saw the layouts, he couldn't hide his pleasure, however grudgingly, at having created this book.

When the book was on press, I heard that Tazio had died in his sleep the night of July 23. In my sadness, I recalled something he had asked me out of the blue one of the last times we had met. "Tell me the truth," he said. "Do you really think there is anything after death?" Concealing my surprise and respecting the effort it must have taken to ask such a question, I cautiously replied yes. I can still see his wry smile. Now, after the timid hesitance of that exchange, I would like to say to him, "Yes, Tazio. I am sure we will meet again."

Diego Mormorio
Rome, July 1998

THE YEARS OF *LA DOLCE VITA*

These and following pages: Anthony Steel (with Anita Ekberg) chases paparazzi on via Veneto

Enrico Lucherini,
Novella Parigini, and
Olghina de Robilant at
de Robilant's party, the
night of the striptease
at Rugantino

These and following pages:
The striptease at Rugantino

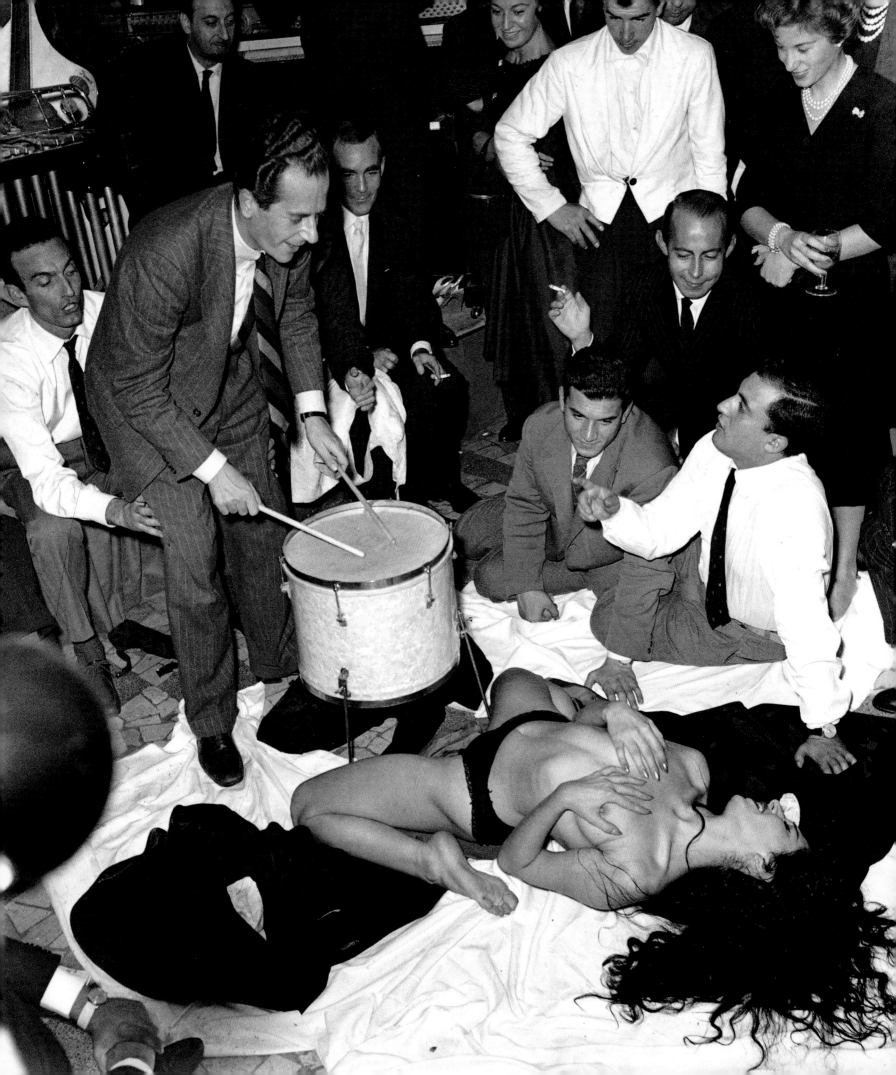

Anna Magnani and Tennessee Williams on via Veneto, August 1958

These and following
pages: The miracle at
Latteria di Maratta Alta
in Terni, June–July 1958

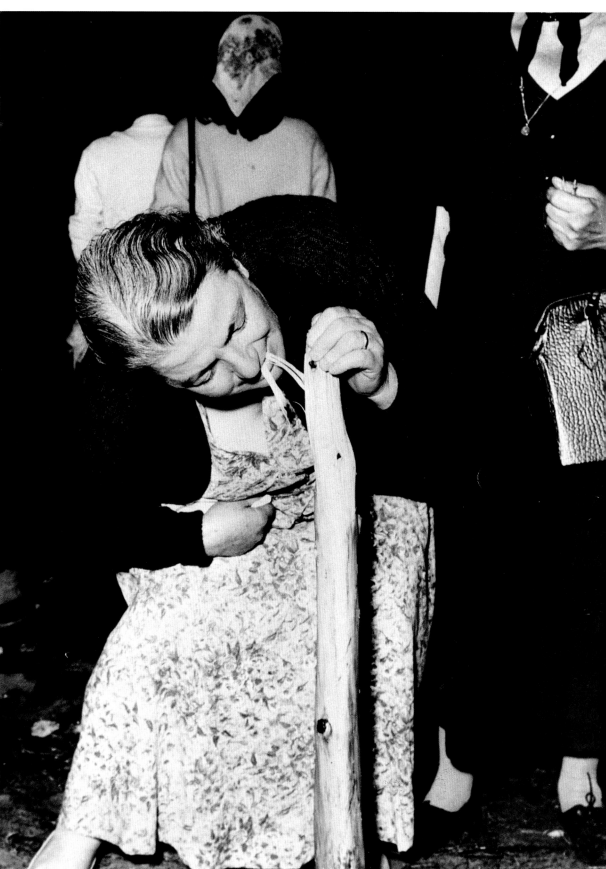

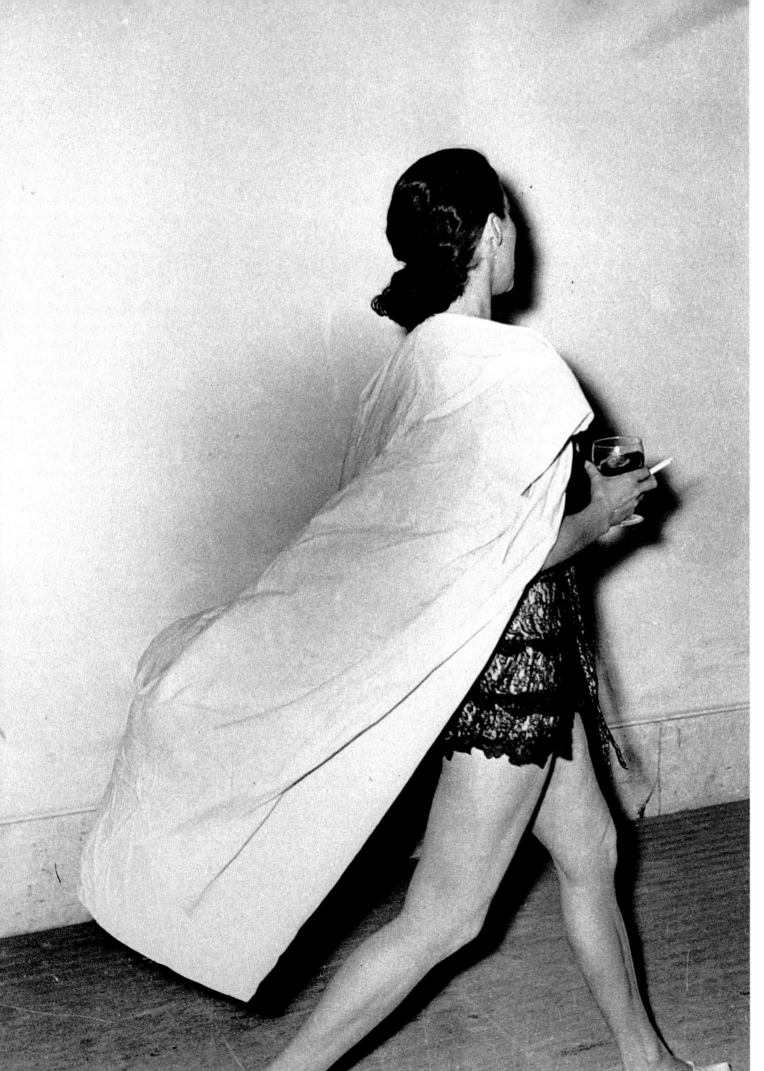

Ava Gardner,
Cinecittà, 1958

David Niven and
Ava Gardner,
Cinecittà, 1958

Right: The photographer
Vittorugo Contino at
Roberto Rossellini's villa

Election of Miss Italy,
July 1954

"Existentialists" at a
little café-bar on via del
Babuino, April 1953

Left: Playing Zingarelli
in Arco di Travertino,
Rome, 1958

Right: Street musicians
on via Sistina,
Rome, 1957

Beggar, Rome, 1953

Beggar, Rome, 1953

Left: Children of the
working class on the
outskirts of Rome,
1955

Right: Ischia, 1957

Balloon vendor, Porta
Pinciana, Rome, 1956

Trinità dei Monti,
Rome, 1956

Demonstration by
young right-wingers at
the Altare della Patria,
Rome, 1956

Clash between young fascists and employees of the Communist daily newspaper *Unità* a few days after Stalin's death, Rome, 1953

Palmiro Togliatti, secretary
of PCI, the Italian Com-
munist Party, at a Festa
dell'Unità (a community
event sponsored by
the local Communist
Party), Rome, 1956

Three members of
Parliament (Lupis,
Saragat, and Romita)
at the Termini train
station, Rome, 1957

THE STARS AND THE EXTRAS

Brigitte Bardot
during a break in the
filming of *Contempt*,
Cinecittà, 1963

Extras at Cinecittà,
1963

Extras at Cinecittà, 1963

Clint Eastwood against the buildings of Cinecittà between takes of *For a Few Dollars More*, 1964

Elsa Martinelli
on the set of
The Tenth Victim,
Cinecittà, 1965

Ursula Andress
on the set of
The Tenth Victim,
Cinecittà, 1965

Virna Lisi, *Casanova '70*, 1965

Ann Turkel Harris
between takes of *The
Cassandra Crossing*,
Cinecittà, 1977

Terence Stamp in *Tre Passi nel Delirio*
Cinecittà, 1967

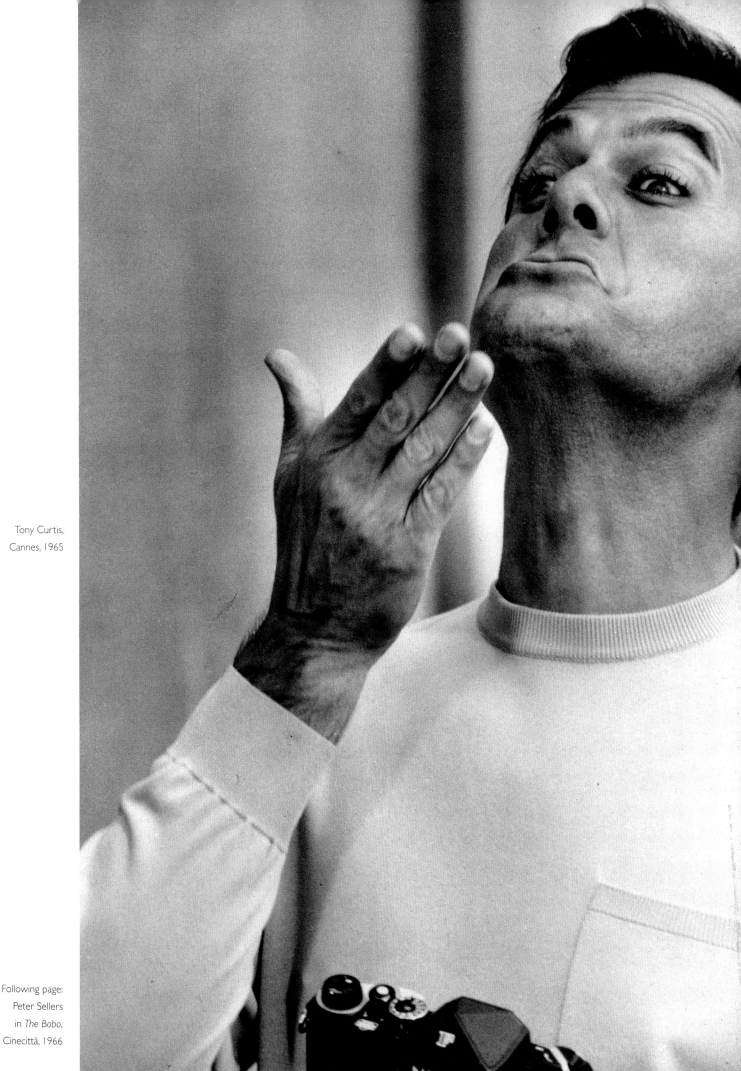

Tony Curtis,
Cannes, 1965

Following page:
Peter Sellers
in *The Bobo*,
Cinecittà, 1966

Sidney Lumet and Anouk Aimée
on the set of *The Appointment*,
Cinecittà, 1969

Eduardo De Filippo and
Marcello Mastroianni rehearsing
a scene for *Shoot Loud, Louder . . .
I Don't Understand*, Cinecittà, 1966

Marcello Mastroianni and Marisa Mell
in *Casanova '70*, Apulia, 1965

Mastroianni during a
break in the filming of
Casanova '70, Apulia, 1965

Mastroianni on the set of *Casanova '70* at Fiumicino airport, 1965

Vanessa Redgrave
with her two children,
London, 1966

Silvana Mangano with her three children on the set of *The Last Judgment*, Teatro San Carlo, Naples, 1961

Britt Ekland jokes on
the set of *The Bobo*,
1966

Raquel Welch in
100 Rifles, Almería,
Spain, 1972

Mastroianni on the set of
The Tenth Victim, Cinecittà,
1965

Following pages: Mina
in a RAI television
broadcast, 1966

Silvana Mangano, 1961

Claudia Cardinale, 1961

Left and right:
Virna Lisi on the set
of *Casanova '70*, 1965

Gregory Peck in *Arabesque*,
London, 1966

David Hemmings
in *Blowup*, 1966

Vanessa Redgrave on the
set of *Blowup*, 1966

David Hemmings
in *Blowup*, 1966

Following pages:
Michelangelo Antonioni
on the set of *Blowup*,
1966

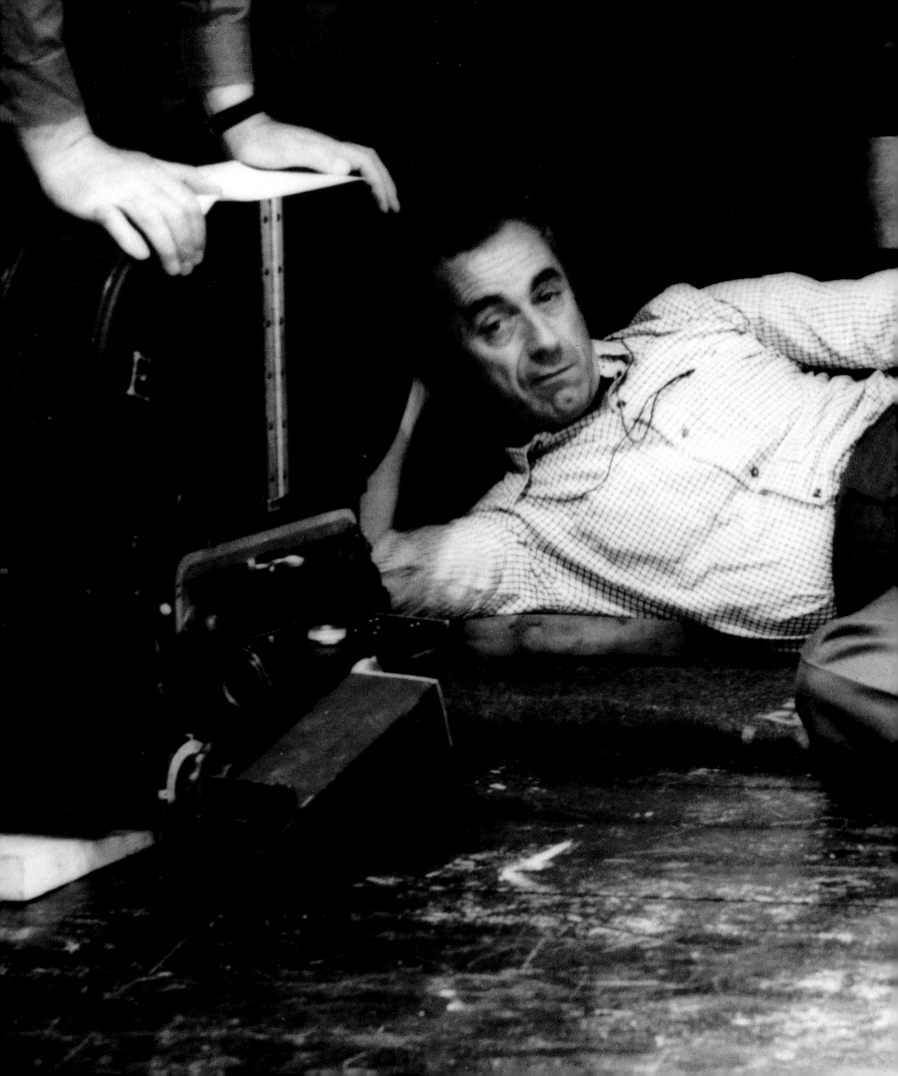

Michelangelo Antonioni
on the set of *Blowup*, 1966

Blake Edwards and Daniela Rocca, accidental double exposure, Cinecittà, 1961

Pier Paolo Pasolini on
the set of *Accattone*,
Rome, 1961

Marco Ferreri
during the shooting
of *Casanova '70*, 1965

Vittorio De Sica
on the set of
Marriage Italian Style,
Cinecittà, 1964

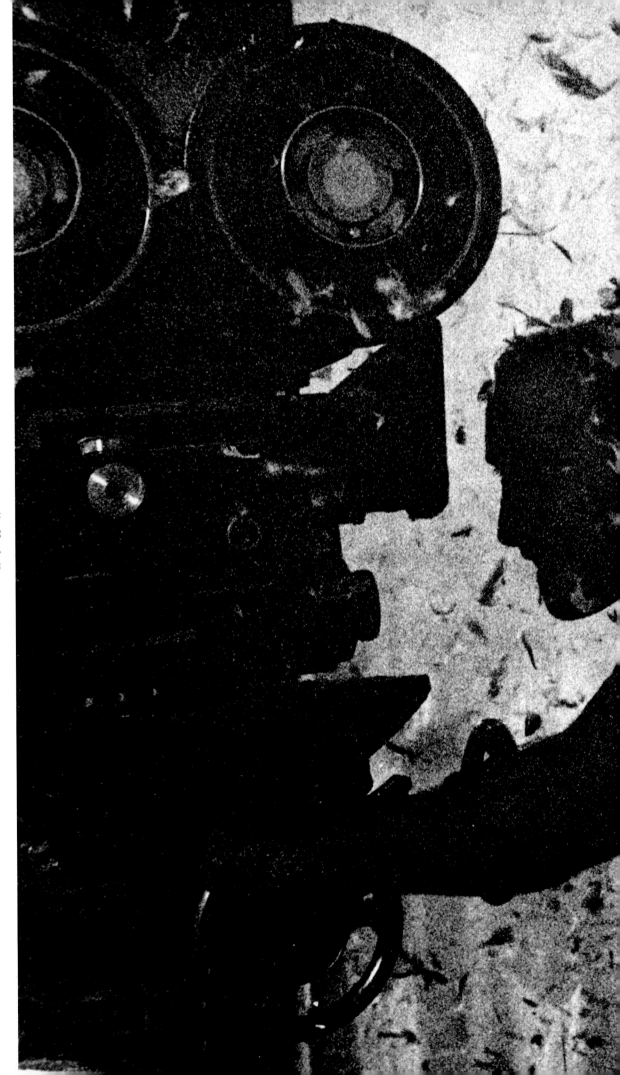

These and following pages:
Federico Fellini during
the filming of *8 ½*,
Cinecittà, 1963

Fellini's shadow,
Cinecittà, 1979

155

Federico Fellini on the
set of *City of Women*,
Cinecittà, 1979

On this and the following pages: Federico Fellini during the filming of *Amarcord*, Cinecittà, 1974

Federico Fellini on the set of *8 ½*, Cinecittà, 1963

Marcello Mastroianni and Federico Fellini joke around on the set of *City of Women*, 1979

Mastroianni on
the set of 8½,
Cinecittà, 1963

Federico Fellini and
Marcello Mastroianni
during a break in the
filming of 8½,
Cinecittà, 1963

Fellini jokes with
Anouk Aimée on the set
of 8½, Cinecittà, 1963

Fellini explains a scene to Mastroianni on the set of *8 ½*, Cinecittà, 1963

Fellini, Mastroianni,
and Anna Prucnal
during shooting of
City of Women,
Cinecittà, 1979

Fellini and Anna Prucnal
on the set of *City of Women*,
Cinecittà, 1979

Fellini explains a scene to Anna Prucnal and Marcello Mastroianni on the set of *City of Women*, Cinecittà, 1979

Fellini on the set of *City of Women*, Cinecittà, 1979

Fellini on the set of *City of Women*, Cinecittà, 1979

Fellini and Mastroianni on the set of *City of Women*, Cinecittà, 1979

Fellini on the set of *City of Women*, Cinecittà, 1979

Fellini and
Sandra Milo on
the set of 8½,
1963

Fellini jokes with
assistant director
Guidarino Guidi
on the set of
8½, 1963

These and following pages:
Federico Fellini and
Marcello Mastroianni on
the set of 8½, 1963

Fellini on the set of
City of Women,
Cinecittà, 1979

Fellini on the set of
City of Women,
Cinecittà, 1979

City of Women, 1979

Federico Fellini,
Cinecittà, 1959

Federico Fellini on
the set of 8 ½,
Cinecittà, 1963

194

Fellini on the set of
Amarcord, Fregene, 1974

Fellini on the terrace
of his house in Parioli,
Rome, 1972

Fellini on the beach
in Rimini, 1974

SIGNORA LOREN

Sophia Loren during
a break between
takes of *Arabesque*,
London, 1966

Following pages:
Sophia Loren and
Richard Avedon,
Rome, 1966

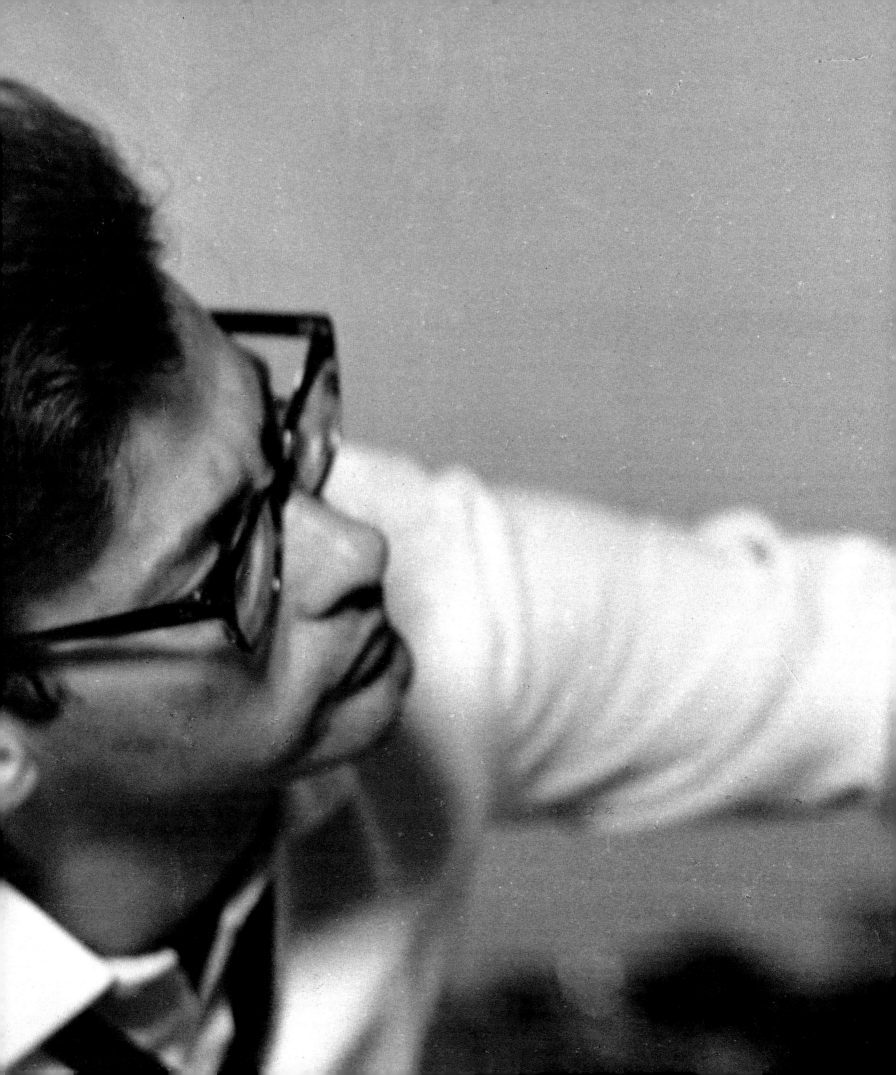

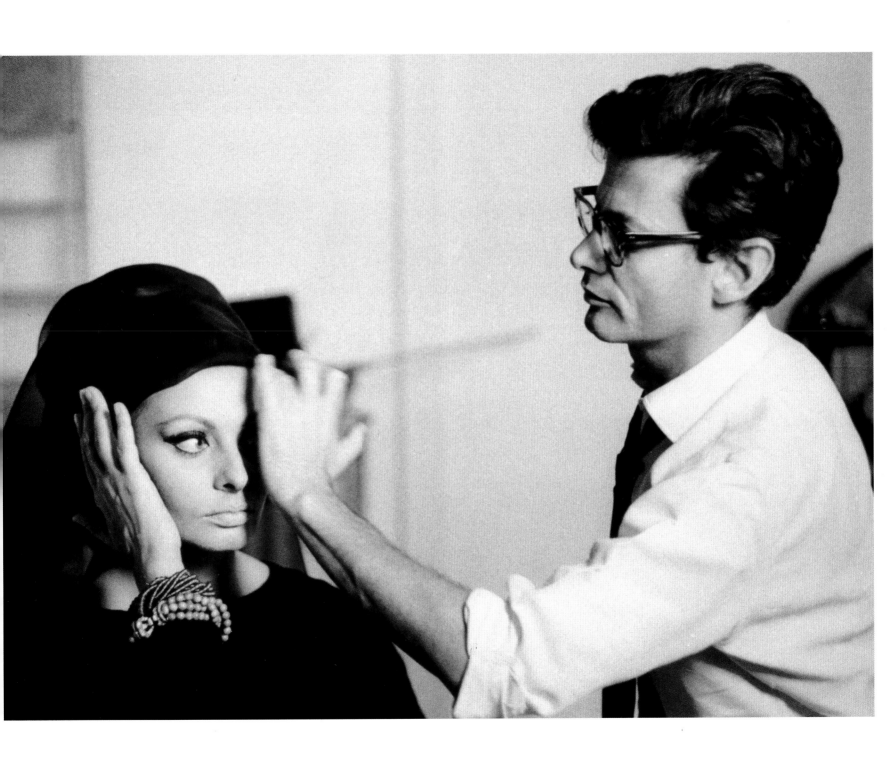

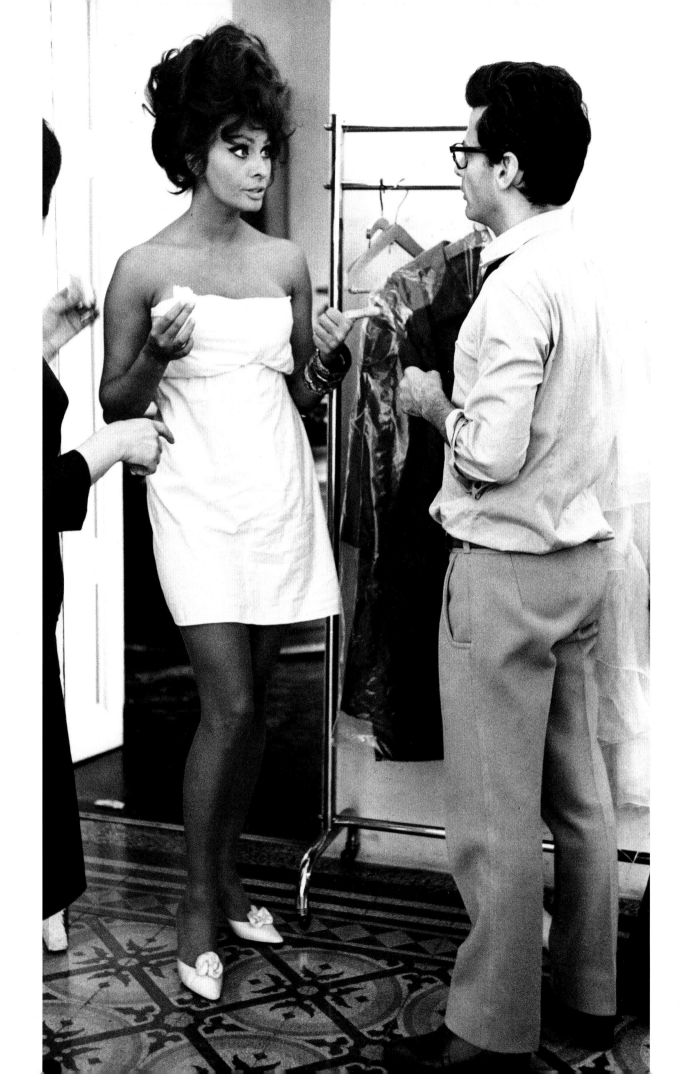

Sophia Loren during a
break in the filming of
Marriage Italian Style,
Cinecittà, 1964

Basilio Franchina,
Vittorio De Sica, and
Sophia Loren during a
break in the filming of
Marriage Italian Style,
Cinecittà, 1964

Charlie Chaplin explains a scene to Marlon Brando and Sophia Loren on the set of *A Countess from Hong Kong*, 1967

Marcello Mastroianni and
Sophia Loren in a scene
from *A Special Day*, 1977

Marcello Mastroianni
and Sophia Loren on
the set of *Marriage
Italian Style*, Cinecittà,
1964

Sophia Loren and Carlo Ponti during a break in the filming of *Arabesque*, 1966

Sophia Loren and
Marcello Mastroianni in
Marriage Italian Style,
1964

Sophia Loren in a scene
from *The Priest's Wife*,
Padova, 1970

Sophia Loren
during the filming
of *C'era una volta*,
Apulia, 1967

Marcello Mastroianni
and Sophia Loren
waiting to shoot a
scene in *Sunflower*,
Milan, 1970

Right
Sophia Lore
in a scene from
The Priest's Wife
Padova, 197

Right and left:
Sophia Loren during a
break in the filming of
The Priest's Wife, 1970

Sophia Loren during a
break in the filming of
Judith, 1966

Sophia Loren on the set of *Arabesque*, London, 1966

Richard Burton jokes with Sophia Loren on the set of *Brief Encounter*, 1974

A little boy enjoys a kiss from Sophia Loren, Wengen, Switzerland, 1978

Sophia Loren signs autographs in London, 1966

Sophia Loren
among the wigs

233

Sophia Loren
during a break in
C'era una volta,
Matera, 1977

Sophia Loren,
Cinecittà, 1966

Sophia Loren jokes on the set of *A Countess from Hong Kong*, London, 1966

Sophia Loren and Carlo Ponti
with their sons in Mégève,
Switzerland, 1976

A little boy digs a hole under the fence to see Sophia Loren on the set of *Arabesque*, 1966

Sophia Loren and
Gregory Peck during a
break in the filming of
Arabesque, 1966

Sophia Loren during
a break in the filming of
Arabesque, 1966

Sophia Loren and
Gregory Peck in
a scene from
Arabesque, 1966

Sophia Loren during a break
in the filming of *Arabesque*, 1966

Sophia Loren during a break
in *C'era una volta*, Matera, 1967

Sophia Loren during a break
in the filming of *Bianco, Rosso e ...* ,
Almería, Spain, 1972

BIOGRAPHY

1925 Born in Rome on November 26 to Marchigian parents.

1941 Takes his first photograph with a friend's 35mm Kodak Retina.

1943 Works as a gofer at Cinecittà.

1944–51 Works as an itinerant photographer on the streets of Rome, taking pictures of American soldiers and tourists. During the summers, he continues doing this on the beaches at Ostia.

1951 Works as a factotum at the International News Service, an American agency in Rome.

1954 Gets his first scoop by photographing an important politician going in and out of a brothel where the man goes to watch his wife make love with other men.
Buys his first Leica.

1955 Founds the Roma Press Photo agency with Sergio Spinelli, whom he met at VEDO.

1958 On the night of August 15, the feast of the Assumption (a major Italian summer holiday), he shoots three photographic features that will initiate the Golden Age of Italian tabloid photography.
Provides Federico Fellini with several cues for Fellini's film *La Dolce Vita*.

1960 Fellini invents the word "paparazzo" while choosing a name for a character in the film *La Dolce Vita*.
The great director opens doors for Secchiaroli at Cinecittà.

1961 Changes his career from paparazzo to set photographer.

1962 Leaves Roma Press Photo to work freelance.

1964 Marcello Mastroianni introduces him to Sophia Loren; he will become her personal photographer.

1964–83 Photographs many international film stars and travels around the world with Sophia Loren.

1979 Is represented at the exhibition *Venice '79. Photography*.

1980 First solo show, at the Palazzo delle Stelline in Monaco.

1983 Ends his career of taking photographs.

1984 At the invitation of Diego Mormorio and Mario Verdone, he conducts an extremely well attended seminar with students of the University of Rome's Institute of the Performing Arts and Sciences.

1990 The Cartiere Milani in Fabriano mounts a solo exhibition of his work.

1996 The Photology gallery in Milan presents an exhibition of his work, *The Original Paparazzo*.

1998 Dies in his sleep the night of July 23.